I
AM
A
SEED

JOURNALING MY WAY TO ME

YVES DOUCET

BALBOA.PRESS
A DIVISION OF HAY HOUSE

Copyright © 2020 Yves Doucet.

All rights reserved. No part of this book may be used or reproduced by any means, graphic, electronic, or mechanical, including photocopying, recording, taping or by any information storage retrieval system without the written permission of the author except in the case of brief quotations embodied in critical articles and reviews.

Balboa Press books may be ordered through booksellers or by contacting:

Balboa Press
A Division of Hay House
1663 Liberty Drive
Bloomington, IN 47403
www.balboapress.com
844-682-1282

Because of the dynamic nature of the Internet, any web addresses or links contained in this book may have changed since publication and may no longer be valid. The views expressed in this work are solely those of the author and do not necessarily reflect the views of the publisher, and the publisher hereby disclaims any responsibility for them.

The author of this book does not dispense medical advice or prescribe the use of any technique as a form of treatment for physical, emotional, or medical problems without the advice of a physician, either directly or indirectly. The intent of the author is only to offer information of a general nature to help you in your quest for emotional and spiritual well-being. In the event you use any of the information in this book for yourself, which is your constitutional right, the author and the publisher assume no responsibility for your actions.

Any people depicted in stock imagery provided by Getty Images are models, and such images are being used for illustrative purposes only. Certain stock imagery © Getty Images.

Print information available on the last page.

ISBN: 978-1-9822-5827-6 (sc)
ISBN: 978-1-9822-5829-0 (hc)
ISBN: 978-1-9822-5828-3 (e)

Library of Congress Control Number: 2020922093

Balboa Press rev. date: 12/02/2020

Artwork by Loretta Gould
mikmaq-artist.com

CONTENTS

Foreword xi
Introduction xiii

Day 1   The Difficulty Is Not Following Your Heart;
        It's Hearing It 1
Day 2   It's the Voices That Trap You, but It's the
        Reflection That Frees You 5
Day 3   It's in the Guaranteed Path We Find Our
        Deepest Pain 11
Day 4   No One Needs to be Fixed; We Need to Be
        Discovered 15
Day 5   The Future Is Easy When You Are Present 19
Day 6   To Stop the Voices, Understand the Pain 23
Day 7   Am I Doing What I Love, or Am I Doing It to
        Be Loved? 27
Day 8   Make Excuses or Be Inspired by the Possibilities 31
Day 9   Life Is Lived in the Choices
        That Move Our Hearts 35
Day 10 An Idea Is Good, but Adding Love Will Make
        It Impactful 39
Day 11 Freedom Is Realizing You Have a Choice 43

Day 12	Every Courageous Choice Is a Step Toward the Heart	47
Day 13	The Choices You Make Will Disappoint Someone—Don't Let It Be You	51
Day 14	Without Listening, Everything Is Based on Ego	55
Day 15	Being You Is So Much Better Than Being Perfect	59
Day 16	Anxiety Goes Away as You Accept Faith	63
Day 17	Going to Your Uncomfortable Emotions Creates a Mind Shift	67
Day 18	Masters Deal with Their Reactions	71
Day 19	It's Your Ego Making You Lonely, Not Your Situation	75
Day 20	It Takes Real Courage to Save Your Own Heart	79
Day 21	Kindness Is a Conscious Decision; Forgive Them	83
Day 22	I Let Go of the Sad and Found Beauty; I Let Go of Beauty and Found My Soul	87
Day 23	The Intention Is More Important than the Business	91
Day 24	Authenticity Is Bigger than Perfection	95
Day 25	Habit Makes You, and Kindness Evolves You	99
Day 26	Once You Understand the Biggest Poverty Is Loneliness, You'll Be Rich	103
Day 27	Stop Trying to Find Yourself; Just Be Yourself	107
Day 28	It's Easy to Love the Winners, but Can You Love the Ones Who Are Trying?	111
Day 29	Be Selfish First, so You Can Serve the Rest of the Day	115
Day 30	You Can't Just Forget About It; You Must Accept It and Understand It	119
Day 31	We Always Have a Choice, but We Rarely Observe That We Have It	123
Day 32	It's in Judgment That We Begin Our Fall	127
Day 33	Be Here because Success Is Not Guaranteed	131
Day 34	Your Change Is Difficult but Beautiful	135

Day 35	Important Trophies Can't Be Shown but Can Be Seen	139
Day 36	Time Doesn't Change Things—You Do	143
Day 37	I Make Time; This Is the Secret to a Great Life	147
Day 38	I Want to Be Part of Something, Not Someone	151
Day 39	Changing Will Make You; Waiting Will Break You	155
Day 40	Dreams Are Your Destinations; the Goals Are Your Plans	159
Day 41	Allow Your Heart to Feel So Your Mind Gathers New Ideas	163
Day 42	To Be Less Reactive, Be More Reflective	167
Day 43	Where You Aim Determines What You See	171
Day 44	I'm More Productive Now That I'm Less Reactive	175
Day 45	No One Is Perfect, Yet We Seek It; Everyone Is Unique, Yet We Hide It	179
Day 46	We May Ask for Your Time, but We Crave Your Energy, Your Attention, and Your Presence	183
Day 47	Don't Let Ego Drive Your Dreams; Let Purpose Make Them a Reality	187
Day 48	Life Is Impossible without Love; Love What You Do, and Love Who You Are	191
Day 49	If You Don't Take a Break, You Will Break	195
Day 50	The Only Way to Escape Is to Change Your Mind	199
Day 51	Leadership Is Not About Taking It Personally but Making It Personal	203
Day 52	The Kinder I Get, the Stronger I Become	207
Day 53	"I'm Not Enough" Is Not a Fact; It's a Reason—Don't Make It Yours	211
Day 54	Don't Focus on Team Building; Focus on Habits of Empathy	215
Day 55	It Feels Like a Life When You Are Present	219

Day 56	Growth Doesn't Happen When You're Right; It Happens When You're Open	223
Day 57	Make Excuses or Be Inspired by the Possibilities	227
Day 58	What You Judge, You Are; What You See, You Become	231
Day 59	You're No Longer Restricted to Where You Are, Only by What You Are	235
Day 60	Opportunity Is Everywhere Once You're Balanced	239
Day 61	I'm Not Who I Want To Be. Will You Love Me Anyway?	243
Day 62	You Can't Give What You Don't Have; Practice Happiness	247
Day 63	Don't Make Me Responsible For Your Happiness; It's Yours to Keep	251
Day 64	I Respect You, So I'll Let You Choose Your Path	255
Day 65	Our Biggest Mistake Is That We Give Our Happiness Away	259
Day 66	I'm Just as Blind as Yesterday, but Today I Know It	263

My Last Message 267
My Last Recommendation 269
Book Recommendations 271
Dedication 273
Acknowledgment 279
About the Author 281

FOREWORD

It's my great pleasure in writing the forward for Yves' first book because he's my best friend, confident, and coach. Without Yves, I wouldn't be the leader I've aspired to be my entire life because I wouldn't have had the ability to see as clearly as I do today. You see, Yves showed me that falling only meant I needed to get back up, that failing only meant I needed a win, and that being broken only meant I needed to heal. It truly was that simple. When I felt like I wasn't worthy, he showed me my worth by giving me pure examples of Love that I shared with the world, and that's Love with a capital *L* because that is what defines us. Lead with Love is our mantra, and we do it without shame; it has everything to do with business and life, and we live it daily.

As you begin to read the short stories of who Yves is, you'll see that the man I call my BFF has a bigger heart than his frame can hold, so he carries it on the outside for us all to see. I know you'll enjoy the journey of journaling and learning to be a better you. Simply allow yourself to fall, rise, fail, win, and Love.

Shelley Butler

INTRODUCTION

> They tried to bury us. They
> did not know we were seeds.
> —Mexican proverb

This quote can be traced back to the Greek poet Dinos Christianopoulos and was popularized by the Mexicans who used it as a catalyst during a civil protest.

This quote had a powerful effect on my transformation, but I soon realized that without acceptance, love, and nurturing, the seed can't grow. This was, in fact, what the poet Christianopoulos realized in his fight for survival. I was able to grow because I got rid of the people who did not fall into those categories, and I surrounded myself with those people who accepted me, like my close friends, those who loved me like my family, and those who nourished me like my coworkers. Shelley is my best friend, and she not only had all three qualities, but she could see the possibility of the seed—of the me who could become that tree.

In 2002 I was fired from the company I helped create. On that day, my friend and business partner decided to sell the company. This resulted in a nine-year court battle where this person tried, and almost succeeded, in burying me. My former partner didn't know I was a seed and didn't know I was surrounded by Love.

As time went by, I grew, and so did my list of friends. They were the reasons I not only survived but can now *be* the acceptance, the love, and the nourishment that other seeds need. What I now realize is that we're all seeds. We need to see our kids as seeds, we need to see our friends as seeds, and we need to see our coworkers as seeds. Once I finally understood that I wasn't here to tell or teach but rather to accept, love, and nourish, I saw the seeds grow.

Taken from the Online Etymology dictionary, the word *consider* comes from the Latin *considerare*: "To look at closely, observe"—to literally "observe the stars." Also, in the late fourteenth century it was defined as "to meditate upon."

I love the word *consider*. It helps us understand without being told what to do but rather to observe, to think about, and to examine our thoughts on the subject. While journaling is a very personal journey, using considerations to explore our lives can be the beginning of the journey.

Consider your truth, consider your thought, consider your emotions, consider your decisions, consider your reactions, consider a better life. Consider journaling as a discovery to a better life. Consider that you are a seed.

One of the best lessons in my life was taken from a book called *The Power of Habit-*; what you do daily more than anything else will influence your future. I built thirty-one daily nonnegotiable habits that are the foundation for my life. I wanted to share one that has changed my life. Journaling helped me identify the most important things in my life and what made me who I am. It helped me start again and grow. It helped me see that I am a seed. It was, to me, the foundation for changing my life because it was the most difficult part—inner reflection. There are many ways to ask yourself deep questions about your behaviors, your emotions, and, ultimately, your decisions, but this is my favorite because writing in a journal has a special effect on your brain. You think, you write, and then you read. These are three ways to input a memory into your brain, and it has a bigger effect on your change than just reading or reflecting alone.

What do you write about? Great question. I will share with you some things I write in my journal and then ask you to consider something in your life. I truly hope that this book of considerations will help you form the habit of journaling.

The second question people ask me: What if someone reads my journal? Well, if they read it and see a human, wrap them up and keep them. If they judge ... It's time to move on.

Lastly, why sixty-six days? Because studies have shown that it now takes an average of sixty-six days to form a new habit. Each daily consideration takes but a few minutes—to read and write—and the importance is on the small daily journaling done, if possible, first thing in the morning. So do it daily, and make this your nonnegotiable. Don't feel you have to fill all the space or follow the rules. There are no rules. There are simply guidelines. Follow your heart. These are small considerations—small bits of nourishment for the seed I see in you.

Thank you so much for your time and energy, and I truly hope this will help you make your life just a little better each day.

Yves Doucet

DAY 1

The Difficulty Is Not Following Your Heart; It's Hearing It

I WAS STUCK in a job I didn't like, but the pay was great, the team was great, and the benefits were amazing. "Be a man and just bear with the pain for a few more years, and then you can retire," I told myself.

The days grew longer, and the amount I needed to retire seemed like an impossible goal. "It's okay," I told myself. "If I just do as I'm told, then I can survive." So I tried to please them—to get better at the things they wanted me to focus on. I tried to get better at reporting my progress and writing and collaborating more with the other teams. Each day grew darker, and my attitude changed, but I didn't see it. I became more defiant and looked to blame others for my unhappiness; I couldn't hear my heart because I was too busy blaming, complaining, and attacking. Pretty soon, I had lost the courage to take on tasks that filled my heart, and as I waited for the others to fail, I was just putting in time.

I had once been very good at innovation, creativity, and selling. I was very good at solving very technical problems, but what I really excelled at was building teams who could deliver world-class products. That was who I could have been. Instead, I became a vice president of nothing. Listening to the critics of others made me try to become like them—or at least what they believed I needed to become—but, more importantly, it blinded me to my true self.

Can you journal about the things you love to do, remembering how they made you feel and how energized you were?

Consider the positive energy you feel as a guide to your path.

I Am a Seed

DAY 2

It's the Voices That Trap You, but It's the Reflection That Frees You

MY DAUGHTER WAS applying for a job with the highest security agency in Canada. They would interview everyone, including myself. There was no doubt that my very public lawsuit would be on the table. My heart felt as if someone had pierced it that day. I wasn't enough; I wasn't a good father. I would be the reason she wouldn't get the job. Triggers come from everyday life events—a friend, a coworker, or, worse, a family member tells you something, and off you go. I could feel the judgment, the criticism—and it infuriated me. It was my trigger into fear. I hit back, but the voices lingered. Days, even weeks—it ruled my head. *I will never be enough; nothing I do is enough.*

Life became slow and oppressive; life became sad. I tried everything to change the relationships with my family, friends and coworker, even stop them, cut them from my life. I ran away, stayed away, and exercised, but the voices just appeared with someone else. The people changed, the places changed, but the triggers remained.

Then I discovered journaling and the power of reflection. Why was I angry? Why did I feel I wasn't enough? I started writing about these subjects and my anger, and I began to accept my emotions. I reflected, trying to understand where and why I was angry and depressed. These voices came from deep in my past, and they ruled my life. They stopped me from being my best self.

I come from a loving home—a privileged life—and I'm grateful. I realize that being born in the right country is also a privilege. If I was loved and suffered no trauma in my childhood, then why did I have these voices?

I started to write down my earliest memories as a child. One memory came back with emotions and clarity: I had gone against my mom's wishes and had accidentally burned a cushion on our fancy couch. I felt shame and never admitted it, even when confronted. This set a narrative that I was an embarrassment to my family and not enough. Deep down in my brain, I was the family embarrassment. If you had asked me at the time, I would have said I was achieving great things. But then why did I feel I had to hide things? Where did the shame and the need to justify my decisions originate?

The joke that life plays on us is this: You will live the life of your subconscious mind. Your reactions will guide you toward making this narrative your reality. Each decision made with logic will bring you closer to this truth. Therefore, we repeat the same mistakes in relationships and in our careers. Simply put, your subconscious mind is the director of your life. The narrative that I was the embarrassment of the family was my guiding narrative; I simply did not know that it was—thus, the joke of life. Living in an unconscious world simply means we're living in our past and can't go any further.

I Am a Seed

The secret you hold and don't know will play out in your life until you have no choice but to confront the real truth. This narrative played out until I lost everything. I was fifty-two years old and had proven myself right. This was reflected to me in my father's words: he couldn't come to stand by me in court because he had a good name and had never been in a fight. The secret, of course, wasn't ready to be revealed, but now I know that I knew nothing. Everything I believed wasn't true; I had to find another truth. To be perfectly clear: I know my father was never ashamed of me and that he loved me with all his heart. This wasn't his narrative—it was mine. The narrative is usually not the truth; it's only the truth as you see it.

The little voices play a big role in our future selves; they are our glass ceilings, and they can't be broken without reflection. What are your voices telling you? Not enough? Not beautiful? What is the dirty little secret you can't admit? Think about this narrative and see if you can find the joke of life: that you don't know that you don't know, so we blame and judge.

My daughter got the job, and I was never interviewed. A few years later, she told me that they asked her the question: "How did the lawsuit and the loss of everything change your dad?"

She replied: "It didn't change him; he is still the same man." I'll remember that moment more than I'll remember my days in the courtroom.

Consider that the voices are not real. What are they saying?

_____
_____
_____
_____

Yves Doucet

I Am a Seed

DAY 3

It's in the Guaranteed Path We Find Our Deepest Pain

> If you're not evolving, you're dying.
> —Marcus Lemonis

It's essential to understand the movement of life because we're taught to be safe and to protect our assets at all costs. In doing so, we lose track of the essence of life; the more we stand still, the riskier life gets.

We're attracted to evolution—to people who reinvent themselves, to people who create new lives. Reading about regrets in life won't bring you to wish you had traveled more, made more money, or worked harder. The regrets will be about the deepest desires in your life you haven't lived. The regrets will be about the love we could not find and the meaning we left undone.

"What if this was the last day of my life? Would I do what I'm about to do today?" I write this question every day in my journal; it was taken from a speech given by Steve Jobs. I don't have any regrets because all I have done, all I have lost, has made me who

I am today. I live my life in the present. I say no to the things that don't move me and say yes to people, places, and things that shift my heart. I live to evolve and leave everyone better than I found them. I may die with no inheritance, I may not have climbed the highest peaks or visited all the great wonders of this world, but I know that tomorrow I will live a different day than today simply because I choose to act and not react. I choose to be present for my family, my friends, and myself. I choose to be creative and change everything I touch for the better. That will be what I leave behind. If I do not share this with those I love, that will be my biggest regret.

Consider the regrets you may have. If this were the last day of your life, would you do what you are about to do today?

_____
_____
_____
_____
_____
_____
_____
_____
_____
_____
_____
_____
_____
_____

I Am a Seed

DAY 4

No One Needs to be Fixed; We Need to Be Discovered

I GET HOME, and Petrie, our dog, jumps up and down. She wants to play. It feels like a long time to her, yet it's only been five minutes. Why is it that our family members aren't as happy to see us? Have we done something wrong? Humans have these narratives—these voices in our heads. We make up stories.

It's interesting that dogs are always happy to see us. It doesn't matter if we have had a bad day or if we didn't do anything that made them proud. They accept us the way we are; they wait for the possibility of a walk, a cuddle, a treat, or just water and a belly rub. Unconditional love. Animals forgive and forget. Humans, on the other hand, remember and try to fix things. Maybe this comes from years of living in a man's world—a patriarchal society where we've forgotten to accept and love one another for who we are.

Here's the joke in life: you can't change anyone except, of course, yourself. And if you change and accept and love others for who they are, then they will follow and be moved by you. Once you see their beauty, you will see yours, and that will move them to change.

Consider that love is accepting others for who they are. Who can you accept?

I Am a Seed

DAY 5

The Future Is Easy When You Are Present

I LOVE INVESTING in the market, and I do well. However, I don't read the papers or listen to the news. I observe. Have you ever looked into someone's eyes for the duration of your conversation? Yes, fifteen, thirty, or even sixty minutes? I mean without looking around, at your phone, or at the interruptions that are walking by? This is what masters understand: you get more insights from presence than you get from your knowledge.

I observe the customers, the service, and the product, and I get a sense of the direction the company is going. You can feel the energy moving it forward or not moving at all. This can't be found in news articles or financial statements, as these are simply measurements of the past.

We judge people by their cars, houses, or clothes; we judge them by their titles and their words. All are simply a mask of the ego of the past and are a poor indicator of the future.

Consider looking at the eyes, the sweat, the energy, the love in their words—their movements. What did you observe?

I Am a Seed

DAY 6

To Stop the Voices, Understand the Pain

IT HAD BEEN two years since I lost my last battle in court, which carried a heavy financial burden. I owed $3 million, and the daily triggers were a constant stress that reminded me I wasn't enough, I wasn't a good father, and I didn't have a good name. My daily workout only served to stop the voices momentarily.

I needed to get the stress out of my life; I wasn't sleeping, and I was in the fight of my life. Life was in a free fall, and I couldn't stop it. I didn't know how to stop it. Exercise was a habit, and it made me feel better. The harder I worked out, the better I felt. The effects didn't last, however, so I did what I needed. I sweated more—some days for three hours. It stopped the voices of despair but only for a short time. This was long enough to do a few things: the first was to learn more, and the second was to fix one small thing in my life—to ask and maybe answer one small question. It would be the smallest step, like pay one bill, the smallest of payment, the smallest movement.

I discovered yoga by chance because all this exercise caused my body to break, which led to the discovery of meditation. The power of just sitting, standing, or lying down ... sometimes walking in peace and remembering the happy places. It was a mini vacation for my brain. Having stopped the voices and on holiday, I could then ask myself deep questions: Why do I believe what I believe? Why am I afraid of being me?

Asking myself questions and seeing the truth helped me understand the suffering. This was a beautiful micromoment that helped stop one of the voices—forever. I understood that the voices are simply a reminder of a hurt or a fear. The voices, which caused the suffering are not the suffering; they are there to prevent pain, and if you don't hear the warning, it will become real as a deeper message. Now I understand that without the habits, I can't stop the voices. I can't hear the warning.

Consider yoga or meditation as a habit to understand your suffering. How did it feel after?

_____
_____
_____
_____
_____
_____
_____
_____
_____
_____

I Am a Seed

DAY 7

Am I Doing What I Love, or Am I Doing It to Be Loved?

I STARTED WRITING a book and actually finished 350 pages of my story. It was hard and did feed my ego; I wanted to be an author and best seller, and I wanted the glory. It's how intellectuals—the smart people—do it. It's how you leave a legacy, so I pushed and pushed and wrote. Then I gave it to a friend (actually to ten friends).

Only one came back with comments. "There should be a law," he said, "against you writing." My friend is a lawyer, so words are his weapon, and they sliced me up pretty good.

So, really determined, I started over. I wanted so much to fit in—so much to be an intellectual. Again, I gave it to ten people, and again, only one came back with comments. Yes, you guessed it: "There should be a law against you writing a book. Consider doing a video book instead," he told me.

It seemed the more I tried to please everyone and fit in, the more I did things that I hated. So I stopped and took my friend's advice and did videos. Some still have negative things to say about my videos, but I don't care. I love doing videos. They feed me, they push my limits, and they help me discover who I am.

I'm doing what I love, and it doesn't matter if I fail because I love doing it. Nothing will stop me. My love gave me the courage to face the possibility of failures.

Consider the emotions you get when you do something you love.
_____
_____
_____
_____
_____
_____
_____
_____
_____
_____
_____
_____
_____
_____
_____
_____
_____

I Am a Seed

DAY 8

Make Excuses or Be Inspired by the Possibilities

WHEN I DECIDED to take a course to become a yoga teacher, I told myself that I was an older man. But I really didn't want to become a teacher. I just wanted to push my knowledge in yoga, which I practice every day. I told myself that I'm a CEO, and CEOs are not yoga teachers. I make good money, and I can never earn that much teaching yoga. I'm very busy, and teaching would be too time-consuming. I can't be a good teacher because I won't put the hours in. That is what I told myself.

Great, I have this! I thought, so off I went to yoga teacher training. When our teacher asked the class why we were there, I raised my hand in excitement. He didn't choose me to share until the next day. By then, I was totally confused, but I stated my case.

He said to me, "Are those reasons or excuses? Why are you here?"

Then I got it—I was afraid. I was making excuses so I didn't fail. I looked deeper for the answer: "To see if I wanted to be a teacher," I said.

He answered, "Great. Now, can you consider the possibilities? Can you see the possibilities?"

This blew my mind. I began looking at the possibilities of how my life would look if I was a teacher and how I could foster a deeper meaning to my life. I started to see how I could share this at work, how I could push my *why* further, and how I could use the messages in my videos and the quotes to give back to my community. I started to see that my stories could help others ask deep questions and how the stories in this book could help others find their own way.

Consider the possibilities without your excuses.

I Am a Seed

DAY 9

Life Is Lived in the Choices That Move Our Hearts

I WAS SO focused on success that I forgot about me. I was so focused on doing a great job that I forgot about my friends, my community, and my family. Without me, there can be no meaning; without them, there can be no community. Without meaning and community, there is no success. I didn't know that the simple truth to success—personal or business—is to do what you love and give that to your community unselfishly, expecting nothing in return.

When you do something out of love, you will have the courage to do the things others will judge and to go toward your fear. When you give your love to your community, you will get what you need in return, and your community will be there to carry you through.

But here's the tricky part—you must do it for ten thousand hours. The first one thousand hours will be difficult, but you will feel amazing, not because you did a great job but rather because you listened to yourself. You should start your day with this small act so that you go to bed fulfilled.

At first, I struggled to find things that moved my heart, so I tried and tried until I found those things. It doesn't have to be complicated. At first, it was simply asking for a double espresso with a smile, which helped the barista have a better day. Then it was small videos on social media, at first once a week and then once a day. Then I added a daily quote. These small expressions of myself have had more impact than any financial contribution I've made to the community. They make me feel, and they make others feel, which is the biggest gift you can ever give. The journey was difficult, but no one said it was going to be easy to have the life I wanted.

Consider doing one thing that moves your heart.

_____
_____
_____
_____
_____
_____
_____
_____
_____
_____
_____
_____
_____

I Am a Seed

DAY 10

An Idea Is Good, but Adding Love Will Make It Impactful

THIS IS SOMETHING you will never hear at a business school: Love is more important than ideas. The intent of your ideas or business proposal is more important than the ideas. I read this great book called *Start with the Why* by Simon Sinek. The book talks about your why in life being more important than your what or how, yet 99.999 percent of all we do starts with the what and then the how. I didn't realize how powerful the statement from Steve Jobs was: "You have to love what you do." This is important because loving what you do will power your doing; it will give you courage and ideas that no one can touch because you will see with different eyes. Before I start or do anything, I ask myself: What is my why? What do I love? What fills my heart?

When I decided to take my yoga teacher training, I asked myself, "Why? Why should a sixty-year-old man who owns a software company take a yoga teacher program?" On the surface, it makes no sense. In my situation, no career consultant would advise me to take that path, and logically, I can't make the connection either. So why do it? Simply because I love the practice of yoga.

So off I went to Tulum, Mexico, with the eyes of a student and ready to accept the possibilities. I arrived open to the possibilities, and it came to me. My why is simple: I want to be the change in business. I want to see business change from a focus on money to a focus on impact—a conscious capitalism. Yoga made me less reactive and more present; it made me more productive and more creative. And teaching yoga was my gift to the community to be the change.

Consider seeking your why in everything you do.

I Am a Seed

DAY 11

Freedom Is Realizing You Have a Choice

I GREW UP believing I was in a free country and that I could do what I wanted. Well, it's true—partially. What I didn't realize was that my choices were influenced by what I read, what I consumed, what my friends were doing and saying, and my fear of not fitting in. I believed I was making choices, but in reality, they were the choices of others.

I did things I didn't really like and then lost my soul watching television or drinking coffee. These things made choices for me, and it was the irony of our social inclusion. Coffee allowed me to go faster without thought or consideration for others. Coffee and my other habits allowed me not to feel or see the humans in my life. My to-do list and my accomplishments gave me permission to disconnect. This was my perception of freedom; I could do as I pleased because I was disconnected. I see this now as sad simply because my reasons guided my choices, but they weren't choices. They were me wanting to have the life of another.

My journey into choices began when I realized that I was being programmed and everything I was told was untrue. I believed in fairness, but I couldn't find it in my business partners. I believed in justice, but the court didn't enforce it. I believed I was a good man, but I didn't see it anymore. Then I started to ask the deep questions about my truth: Who am I? What do I love? What is my meaning in life? Why can't I feel anything? These questions led me to one answer: my heart.

To have choices and freedom, I had to find my heart. I had to feel and give and fall in love with the life I was creating, one choice at a time. It wasn't easy. Each decision came with guilt, judgment, and pain, but eventually, I found my heart and, behind it, my truth and freedom to be present.

Consider the choices you can make to change your life.

_____
_____
_____
_____
_____
_____
_____
_____
_____
_____
_____
_____

I Am a Seed

Yves Doucet

DAY 12

Every Courageous Choice Is a Step Toward the Heart

I WAS ASHAMED—THE black sheep of the family. I'd lost everything and needed to borrow from my family to pay for mistakes. This left me in deep, dark places. I never believed life would get this dark. *To err is human. I'm not a bad guy,* I kept silently repeating to myself. That didn't do enough to rid my suffering or convince me. So I took my courage into my habits and decided to walk in front of the office of my partner—the one who had left me to die.

It felt better as I honored my words. *I have nothing to be ashamed of,* I told myself. Then I sat down for a coffee next to his office. Wow! I felt so much better. As it turned out, there is scientific data on this. If I ran away, thus putting action into my fear, it made the fear real. To the brain, the fear is now real, and the narrative that I'm the shame of the family is true. The smallest step of courage opened my heart.

It was a small step because I was afraid that I was going to see him. It was six o'clock in the morning, and no one was up except me and the nice barista. Nevertheless, it gave me the courage to face my day and open my heart.

Consider taking a physical step going closer to face someone who has hurt you.

I Am a Seed

DAY 13

The Choices You Make Will Disappoint Someone— Don't Let It Be You

WHAT WILL MY parents think? What will my friends think? How will this look on my resume? How will my community judge me if they know? These are great scary questions and all great reasons not to do what you love to do. I still get stuck in life by these questions, even at sixty.

It's ridiculous how trying to fit in is so ingrained in our DNA. It was necessary for our survival. If we did not have this programmed into our genes, our communities would send us into the woods in exile, and it would be painful. We've survived because we had communities.

The worst thing you can do to another person is make them irrelevant or remove your love. This is like exile and has the effect of leaving the person all alone. We use this in our relationships and in our companies; when we escort our long-term employees out the door and tell them not to contact customers and employees, we place them in exile.

They put me in exile. It was so lonely to be apart from my friends who did not dare contact me for fear of reprisal. I spent ten years working for a company that I helped create, and then my friend and partner told me I was done without explanation. In actuality, he didn't do it, he stayed home that day. This man I hardly knew told me not to contact my friends and told my friends not to contact me. He told me that they would send my things. He said I shouldn't worry; it wasn't personal. It felt as if I were dead. Running into my old friends felt different, as if they were doing something wrong. I could feel the shame inside of me each time I saw them—the shame that I had become.

It took me some time to understand my feelings that day—the power to belong, the power to have meaning, and the power to make others irrelevant.

Today when I make a choice that may be viewed by my community as a disappointment, I tell them and try to make sure they understand that I'm not moving away. I'm still there and still care for them deeply. I understand that my choices are mine, but others can see them as me moving away from them, so I make sure they know my intentions. I understand that even when I chose to let go of a friend or a coworker it was for my own path with no judgment on them. I make sure they know that I appreciated our personal relationship. I'm honest about the great moments we shared and the importance they have played in my life. It was a moment in my life, and my path has changed. I do it for them but also for me, so I can go and be the best I can. I now understand that not making things personal is really an excuse to feed my ego. To not make it personal hurts them at the moment but allows me to hide my dirty little secret from myself.

Consider letting go with compassion. Whom do you need to let go?

Yves Doucet

DAY 14

Without Listening, Everything Is Based on Ego

I LOVE GIVING back to my community; I started giving time, coaching, or just talking (mostly listening). This has been so rewarding as I meet so many amazing humans. My friend Alex, thirty-five years my junior, wanted to talk, and after six months or so of meeting regularly, he asked if he could practice his coaching on me. In return, he asked if I would consider giving him a recommendation if he did a good job. I accepted, but to be frank, I was a bit dubious. I am, after all, older and a CEO, and I have had a life of experience and training. I follow the best coaches in the world. How could this young man help me?

Alex asked me a simple question: "Where is the one space you need help?"

Well, nowhere, I guess. The more I thought about it, the more reasons I had. I'm a coach too. I'm so grounded, so zen, that I'm almost a master. Right?

Then it hit me. Those were all reasons—excuses. They were reasons not to be open and not to listen. So ... I let them go. It took some time, but I let them go. Finally, I could ask him for help. "Can you help me turn off my ego? Can you help me listen and be more here—more present?" Well, Alex blew me away with his wisdom and guidance. I now see the possibilities—the possibilities in the letting go.

Consider that your ego is simply a stream of reasons. Consider letting them all go. List your excuses.

I Am a Seed

DAY 15

Being You Is So Much Better Than Being Perfect

I TAUGHT MY first yoga class this morning, and it was far from perfect. I missed cues, the instructions were not precise, I slurred words, and I spoke too softly. It wasn't perfect. As I was preparing for my class, I began with my intention. Why was I here? Why was I doing this? My intention was to leave this world a little better—to leave people feeling a little better about their possibilities.

So here I go ... Class starts, and halfway through the class, the music stops, but I move on. I lead the class with my intention: "My intention today is ..."

Nothing. I start laughing—this silly, almost sinister laugh. I'm thinking my intention is really to make them sweat, but I can't say that, so I continue the practice and continue to find myself funny and silly.

Finally, I can say it out loud. "My intention is to make you consider the possibilities."

After class, not one person said, "You missed a cue," or "The music stopped," or "The instructions were wrong." They did say, however, that the practice was an expression of my personality—the laugh, the instructions, the intention, and the practice. They did say, "I needed this today and will come back."

It wasn't perfect, but it was me.

Consider not taking yourself too seriously. Where did you judge yourself, and can you laugh at it?

I Am a Seed

DAY 16

Anxiety Goes Away as You Accept Faith

I'M WALKING INTO the office, and there are two sheriff cars in front of our building. My heart goes cold, and I tremble. They're here to seize the company assets—they're here for me. With every phone call, every police car, every time I arrived home anticipating another registered letter, I felt the fear of the unknown—the fear that I couldn't stop this and that I had no more control over any aspect of my life. This was difficult for someone who had his life plan set in stone.

The more I tried to fix it or control it, the more exhausted I became. I was living in constant fear of living, where staying in bed was nice and easy.

One day I decided to just go see the sheriff, bring him a coffee, and invite him to my home. I wasn't trying to control or change anything; I was just tired of waiting. I discovered that he was a nice man, and he just had a job to do. He understood my fears. This didn't solve my problem, but I was less anxious because I knew he would call me if he needed something. Every time I felt anxious, I would go see him to find out if he needed anything from me. I started to do the same things with all my creditors, and I felt better. I had accepted that life will happen. There was no way I could pay all my creditors today, but I could pay a little at a time.

What would happen tomorrow if I could not pay? That was just tomorrow, so I let it go. I could only be here today, and I could only do the here and now. I let go of trying to control every little thing and was simply open to the present. Because I didn't know what would happen tomorrow, I let go of trying to figure it out. I had a plan, but I let it go every day to be present.

Consider that you can't control the future.

_____
_____
_____
_____
_____
_____
_____
_____
_____
_____
_____
_____
_____
_____
_____

I Am a Seed

DAY 17

Going to Your Uncomfortable Emotions Creates a Mind Shift

I'VE BEEN JOURNALING now for several years and recently added a review component to my journaling. I simply take a past journal and write two pages of that past into my present. This exercise made me realize that I was stuck in the same problems and the same emotions. I wasn't living. I was repeating the same day over and over. Yes, the actors had changed, the scenery had changed, but I hadn't changed.

I became sad and lonely, wondering, *How can this be? I'm working so hard at having a beautiful life. Why am I still at the same place, saying the same things? My friends must find me boring. I have the same complaints, the same arguments, the same me.*

I started to reflect and write about my truths—my reasons for complaining and blaming. I also started asking why. This is when things started to change—when I started to change: when I could admit my truths, my deepest shame, and my deepest fears. Once I could accept these truths—that I was just a human in a human world—I saw the world differently. I saw the possibilities. They were possibilities of change and a life where everything was a choice and a possibility. The miracle of my life lived in my truth.

Consider reviews and reflections of past events to discover your truths.

I Am a Seed

DAY 18

Masters Deal with Their Reactions

I WAS TRYING to read but found it impossible with the noise on the street from those awful hogs—old white men trying to find their youth and look cool. *Don't they realize they are disturbing everyone?* I wondered. *I should make a complaint to the city to bar the noise so that it becomes a better community.*

Then I realized that they're the majority; they're actually the community. Not too long after this, I was at a conference where one of the speakers had a similar experience in a taxicab playing loud music. The speaker suggested that we voice our opinions and ask the cab driver to turn down the music. "It was disrespectful and didn't honor the passenger," he continued. "We should say something, and we should make our voices heard. We should set boundaries to protect ourselves."

However, this didn't resonate with me so much; it felt unnatural to impose my views on others. I'm not saying the taxi driver or the noise machines are great behaviors, but neither is imposing rules on others' ways of living. The speaker continued his talk, and then a phone rang in the audience. He stopped his talk and asked that everyone please turn off their phones. It was disrespectful, and I agree that it was, but could he have continued regardless of the noise?

I guess my focus is less about controlling life and others' lives and more about becoming a master. Olympians don't ask people to shut their phones off or not to take pictures; they get into their flow with focus (*drishti*) and do the job. Then everyone becomes fixated on the art of flow—the art of removing noise and doing what you must even with the noise.

Masters focus on their emotions and deal with the reactions by getting them more in focus—more into their flow and into their art. When they do, they change the community and the behaviors of those around them simply because others are mesmerized by their focus and their performance. Let's face it—we all want to be Olympians at our lives.

Consider that you must focus in the most turbulent times to become a master.

I Am a Seed

DAY 19

It's Your Ego Making You Lonely, Not Your Situation

I FELT SO lonely. It seemed like the more I focused on doing what I liked to do instead of what everyone else wanted to do, the more I was doing those things alone or with new friends. The more they asked me to go golfing, the more alone I became. So I decided to go for a hike in the woods—for four days.

It was the end of October, and here in Atlantic Canada, it's a bit chilly. -5 degrees C at night and reaching 8 degrees C during the day. I was going alone and sleeping alone, and it wasn't going to be an easy seventeen peaks and valleys. But I needed to go.

I had enough battery power and coffee for four days and even brought a little flash of courage. The phone was important because I wanted to listen to audio books. I saw no one during those four days, but I listened to *The Meaning of Life* by Viktor Frankl. The author talked about life in concentration camps, where life happened and the more he tried to control it, the worse it got. This letting go of the control and having faith in life was a story that made me cry. My air mattress wasn't holding its air, and

I ran out of fuel for my stove, but it paled in comparison to what the concentration camps were like, so I let it go and continued.

I listened to Brené Brown's book called *Braving the Wilderness*. I learned about the power of setting boundaries and accepting my emotions as my truth. It started to rain very hard, so instead of getting mad at the weather, I took a shower outside. It was my first shower in three days, and it felt amazing.

Then it was time for Marianne Williamson's *Tears to Triumph*. She talks about loneliness and how most people are lonely even when they're in a room full of people. It was getting cold, and I had missed the tide, so I was stuck on the riverbank, waiting alone and frozen. I made a fire and listened to nature. My batteries had almost run out. Then I realized I wasn't alone. I loved my friends and family, and I needed to finish my work to give back to them. Love was a gift to them, not from them. Then it all made sense—I was alone but not lonely. *My loneliness came from not loving myself enough to have faith.* I felt warm and energized. I was no longer alone. I saw the love in others that I hadn't seen before.

Consider that your ego is the reason you're lonely. Can you see love in others?

_____

_____

_____

_____

_____

_____

_____

_____

I Am a Seed

DAY 20

It Takes Real Courage to Save Your Own Heart

I'M A MAN ... not the best candidate for emotional living. I was trying to be perfect, a strong leader; my team, my family, my son, and my daughter all needed me to be strong. Most days brought me to my knees, and I cried in silence. I didn't want to be strong or the hero; I wanted to stay in bed.

I hid my feelings and felt less and less. Was this my life? I cared less about everything. Work was just another day to nowhere. *How can I feel? How can I live like this?* I wondered. This quest for perfection was impossible, and I'd had enough.

I started to give hugs, and I stopped trying to be perfect; I decided I was just going to be me. I guess I could do this now because my life became so gray that I didn't care what others thought or believed. Why wouldn't I just be me? I was going to hug at work, and I was going to hug my dad. These small acts of courage led me a little closer to opening my heart, to caring, to being a leader, and to being me. It turns out no one wants a perfect leader; we all only want a *human* leader.

Consider how a hug makes you feel, and then go out and give some.

I Am a Seed

DAY 21

Kindness Is a Conscious Decision; Forgive Them

THE PHRASE *TO forgive* comes from the word *perdonare* in Latin: "to give completely." It's a gift without intent that you give to others and eventually a gift for you. What I didn't realize was that in order to forgive others, I had to see them as humans.

I fought my friend for ten years in court and lost. Although he won, I'm sure it wasn't easy because fighting is never easy for anyone. But I didn't like him too much, and I blamed him for what he had done. I gave him the best years of my life, worked very hard to make the company a success, dedicated my best hours, and sacrificed my friends and family. How could he treat me that way, like a stranger, so impersonal, so inhuman?

I couldn't understand until I started to see him as human—his fears, his pain, and his reactions to my behavior. I started to question my responsibility in things and then started to see him in me. I saw the great times we had during those first ten years of building a business. I became conscious of my reactions and unconscious behavior. He stayed home because he was afraid of me; it was just a reaction to his dirty little secret. I saw that I also had a secret. We all do.

The hurt went away because I realized he was trying to do the best he could to survive. So I gave him a gift: I forgave him, and I was free.

Forgiveness is never for the other person. Forgive them because letting anger and revenge run your life is like letting those you hate live in your brain rent-free. I gave him a book and wrote this note:

> *Jon, despite our differences of the past, the one thing I will remember is our great discussions about business and technology. Great books, like this one, were always the pinnacle of our discussions. I truly hope you enjoy it, and I wish nothing but happiness in your life.*
>
> *Yves, July 5, 2016.*

Consider seeing the people who make you angry as only human. Consider forgiveness.

_____
_____
_____
_____
_____
_____
_____
_____

I Am a Seed

DAY 22

I Let Go of the Sad and Found Beauty; I Let Go of Beauty and Found My Soul

I HAD TO let go of the darkness. Everything reminded me of how people were greedy and were just looking out for themselves, not others. It made me angry and sad. But here's the thing: time goes quickly when you're angry and slowly when you're sad.

I turned off the news, radio, and television; I stopped reading the papers; and I didn't consume any social media. It worked temporarily, but then I still saw people; they had opinions they didn't see or understand. That made me mad and then sad. Would I have to go live like a hermit? I spent more time alone, reading, learning, and asking myself deep questions. When I finally let go of the sad, it was just in my head—a world I had made up. Then I got pulled into the beauty, the trophies, the titles, and the glory of being me. This too I found was a construct of my mind. I wasn't that good. I should get over myself. I gave away my title; I gave away my trophies. The pretense was that I knew more and that

I was more. It was then that I found my soul. It was no worse or better—just me.

Consider letting go of your titles, your trophies, and your pretenses that feed your ego. Consider feeding your soul instead.

I Am a Seed

DAY 23

The Intention Is More Important than the Business

THE VISION IS more important than the business. The intention of the business is more important than the actual business. This seems pretty straightforward, but we get lost in the rules, guidelines, and politics. We just launched a new program in our business called Courage. The intention of the program is to find your courage. The rules are simple: every employee, once every two years, can spend up to $3,000 on finding courage.

The first question was: What are the rules or guidelines? My answer was simple: The intention is more important than the rules. The intention of the program is the name of the program. "What is the intention of courage?" I asked. "Courage."

This is simple. We make life difficult and complicated. We start with intentions, then we make rules, and that's why we have more than 250,000 rules in our province. Yet, we have lost our intentions. That's why the court is full of people who test the rules, and we can't find justice because we've lost the intention behind the rules. We spend very little time on intent.

Martin Luther King didn't say, "I have a goal: He said, "I have a dream." He had intent. Intent drives movements. It gives hope, produces innovation, and fills your imagination.

What's the intention behind your life rules? What's your intention behind how you save or spend money? What's your intention behind your diet or exercise? Is it a goal or an intention? Is this intention created by ego or by meaning?

Consider creating an intention for your smallest of movements.

I Am a Seed

DAY 24

Authenticity Is Bigger than Perfection

I PUBLISH A video daily. It's a one-minute video with the intent to share my journey to creativity with the community I love. On a good day, I have twenty-five likes and one share. If I start to compare myself to others, I'm a failure. They have youth, they have grace, and they have beauty. It's not fair. I use filters and try to use that perfect angle, but it doesn't work, and I can't compete against beauty. So I decided to be me—authentic.

I am as real as I dare, and then something beautiful happens … I don't get more likes or shares. Life doesn't work that way. I get more impactful, I get more friends, and I get more life. The more I give of myself without intent but with authenticity, the better life gets. I discover belonging; I discover peace and possibilities.

Consider being you instead of trying to be perfect or like someone else.

Yves Doucet

I Am a Seed

DAY 25

Habit Makes You, and Kindness Evolves You

I HAVE THIS wonderful friend who lives in Russia. She asked me about my daily habits. I mention this because we're no longer restricted by where we are but by who we are. I sent her my habits, including my thirty-one non negotiables.

Then she asked, "Did you arrive at this all at once, or have you always been a habit guy?"

Well, no. I just started doing these eight years ago when I fell hard. I understood at that time the saying, "Stand for something or fall for anything." I hadn't stood for much other than myself and earning money. This led to my crash, and I had to start over. From the book *The Power of Habits* by Charles Duhigg, I also understood that your habits dictate your life. I started with no newspaper, no radio or television. This simple habit took more than one year to implement. Everyone around me believed I was nuts.

What would I talk about if not television programs or the news? My friends would ask, "Did you see the game last night?" No. "Did you see they elected a new president?" No. "Did you watch that new episode of *So You Think You Can Dance?*" No.

It was embarrassing and difficult. But soon, we started talking about life and what we loved and our opinions. We started talking about real things and having true conversations without filler. Now I had more time and started my second habit: exercise.

As the list grew longer, I saw a change, but it was when I hit number twenty-four—#BeccaToldMeTo be kind—that I evolved. Becca was a young girl who had been diagnosed with terminal cancer.

When her parents asked what she wanted, she said, "For everyone to be kinder." She started the movement #BeccaToldMeTo as a way for people to share their small acts of kindness. I started doing small acts of kindness every day, and my heart grew. What I didn't expect was that my brain changed … I became more open and more creative in ways to give but also in my life.

Consider random acts of kindness you can perform in order to evolve. What can you do to be kind?

_____

_____

_____

_____

_____

_____

_____

I Am a Seed

DAY 26

Once You Understand the Biggest Poverty Is Loneliness, You'll Be Rich

JON AND SUE, whom I once called friends and partners, turned out to be my demise. We once laughed, and then we fought to the end until one or all of us died metaphorically. What was my biggest financial opportunity would turn out to be my worst mistake and my biggest lesson. We built an amazing company and products together only to let our collective ego destroy everything good about what we had done. All that was left after our court battle was the money. They had it all. I had nothing—nothing, that is, except the most valuable of things, the most valuable of power. I was left with the lesson of my life.

They took all the money I had, which took me a lifetime to accumulate—fifty-two years to be exact. They took my title; they even took my name. They accused me of being a bad employee who cheated, lied, and was greedy. They did it in public to disgrace my name and make me the shame of my community and, worse, of my family. They published in the local papers and sent the sheriff to collect what was left. They warned all my coworkers that they were not allowed to talk to me, and as the last coup de grâce, they convinced a judge that this was all true. Justice was that I would go bankrupt with no chance of getting out before ten years had passed.

They tried to bury me, and they did, deep, never to be seen or heard again. But they didn't know I had friends and family who didn't believe the accusations and wouldn't abandon me. Not once did my friends and family leave me lonely; not once did they make me feel like I was less. Every day they gave me water and sunshine; they knew I was buried, and all I needed was water, sun, and some love.

They were right. I was a seed. All I needed was to feel warm and to be given some food of hope. The worst thing you can ever do to someone is say they don't matter. When my partner testified in court that I wasn't his friend, he didn't recall me, I was just an employee, he buried me.

Consider your words to feed those seeds in your life. What can you say to someone that is kind?

_____

_____

_____

_____

_____

_____

_____

_____

_____

I Am a Seed

DAY 27

Stop Trying to Find Yourself; Just Be Yourself

I WANTED TO know who I was. I wasn't the vice president, I wasn't the engineer, and it seemed I wasn't the father I thought I was. Lies seemed less complicated. No one needed me, but how could I be anything for my son and daughter? I had no money and no power. I was nobody.

So I started walking alone in the woods. What did it matter anyway? Somewhere away from them, I would find myself on this vacation from living a life I didn't believe in. I discovered that the more I tried to get away, the more I was still there. The problems and the narratives continued.

So I stopped running and dug in. I dug into me—what and where was I? Who was I?

What did I love? What and who inspired me? Where did I matter? It wasn't easy or fun, but then I got it: It wasn't a question. It was a movement. It wasn't, "Who am I?" It was, "What do I love?"

I found who I was meant to be by doing the things that light up my life. It was just accepting myself.

Consider what you love.

I Am a Seed

DAY 28

It's Easy to Love the Winners, but Can You Love the Ones Who Are Trying?

I WAS VERY proud when my daughter graduated from university and when I attended my son's launch party for his new business. That was easy. But can I be proud when they get hit? Can I resist protecting? Can I just be the water they need or the sun they seek?

This is the hardest job I've ever had ... to be a father, to see my children fall, to resist protecting them, and to watch them get up.

Nothing, and I mean nothing, brings me to my knees as hard as watching my kids—my loved ones—fail. Just writing this brings me to my knees. Yes, I'm crying just thinking about it.

I need courage not to act—not to overact; this is the most difficult part of life I've come to learn. This is what takes the most courage: to love, to give them water, and to hug them. This is real courage. This is truly being a human being.

Consider the beauty in just trying; we may fail, but we'll get back up. What can you observe without judgement with the ones you love?

I Am a Seed

DAY 29

Be Selfish First, so You Can Serve the Rest of the Day

THERE'S A BOOK I read a long time ago called *The Wealthy Barber*, which explains the easiest way to become a millionaire. The concept is easy: pay yourself first, small daily amounts, invest these amounts into an account that accumulates interest, and the effect of compound interest will eventually grow exponentially. The author says to pay yourself first. Take the ten dollars you saved on that latte this week and save it in an interest-bearing account.

This concept is the same for your happiness. You must pay yourself first. The first thing you do in the morning should be to invest in something you love doing. That way, at the end of the day, you'll look back and say, *"Yes, I did something for me."*

I started small with fifteen minutes a day, but eventually, this investment started to show potential. So I invested more. It grew to one hour every morning and then eventually to the entire morning and then the full day. Today, because of that small daily investment in me, I do what makes me happy every day, all day.

Consider investing in yourself first.

I Am a Seed

DAY 30

You Can't Just Forget About It; You Must Accept It and Understand It

I FELT LIKE I wasn't enough. I felt that I wasn't a good man or a good father. Not being able to support my family and bring home enough for them was a devastating time in my life. I was trying to forget but couldn't. Being human, I tried to control it—my emotions and the reactions to my energy. My habits helped, but the smallest of things sent me in a downward spiral toward my own failure.

So then I started to accept it, to rest when I needed, and to reflect on the triggers that brought me to despair. It could be the smallest of things: a word, a look, even if I saw someone who looked like my fears. So why did I think the way I was thinking? I peeled the onion. I blamed my dad, my loved ones, and others for making me feel like I wasn't enough. This gave me some relief because it wasn't my fault. Right?

Then off I went to learn to be a yoga teacher, and my teacher took me through a process of discovery of the real narrative—my dirty little secret. I was simply playing out my narrative. As I mentioned earlier, as a child, I had burned a cushion on the fancy couch and hid it from my family. I was the shame of the family, and I was making this story come true again. I finally understood the narrative that guided my life and made me. That broke me.

Consider what you can't understand. What habits are your trying to break? Consider the feelings after doing them. Can you write about past events that had the same feelings?

I Am a Seed

DAY 31

We Always Have a Choice, but We Rarely Observe That We Have It

I THOUGHT I had a choice in deciding to sue my partner. No, he wasn't fair, and he didn't honor his word. I believed that I made the choice from logic and sound thinking. This is so funny now, looking back, because I didn't know. I didn't know that I didn't know. I was blind to the realization that my mind was playing me. My reality was that I was the shame of the family and I was going to prove to them that I was right, but I didn't know I was doing this. I didn't realize that I didn't know. My subconscious mind was guiding my decisions; my ego was playing the game. I believed I was justified in my attacks, but they were only justified by my ego and my narrative.

These acts would continue until I proved my subconscious right—that I was the shame of the family. My reactions to life were going to make me fail, and my ego was going to ensure that every decision I made wasn't guided by logic but rather by ego. I understood that I was attacking too much, that I was accusing too much, and that I was going too far in my pursuit of what I wanted to call justice, but I ignored the observations of that feeling, thinking logically. I had the evidence, I had the law, and we lived in a just society. What I didn't observe was the world around me. I was blind to the effects to the true reality. I was blind to the opportunities because I wasn't living in the present. I was living in the past.

Every time I got closer to being a success in life or a relationship, I figured out that I was going to give up or I was going to decide that I was going to prove myself right. This decision was simply an ego decision. It wasn't a conscious choice. It was done with my ego. I couldn't see it, I couldn't observe my ego, and I couldn't see that I was going to be right.

Consider observing your emotions instead of using logic as a tool to decide. How do you feel, and what do you do when you feel this way? Can you see the patterns?

_____
_____
_____
_____
_____
_____
_____
_____
_____
_____
_____
_____

I Am a Seed

DAY 32

It's in Judgment That We Begin Our Fall

MY FRIEND—MY BOSS—STARTED to criticize my behavior. This, of course, was upsetting. Who was he to tell me what to do? He simply sat in his office while I was doing the work, building the product, attending the endless meetings with the customers, and traveling constantly. I was the one putting in the ridiculous hours and taking the calls at all hours of the day, every day of the week. I believed I was better than him, more intelligent, and harder working; therefore that made me more powerful. That's when it started.

Judging was just a reflection of my ego, and it made the decisions. It decided that I would wait until he did his job, and then I would make fun of him and belittle him for his Dilbert style of management. It made the decision to play less, wait, and say less. It made the decision to take him to court.

I wasn't observing my emotions or my ego. If I had been observing, I would have seen my reaction to his behavior. Yes, I had choices, but I couldn't see that I could leave and continue my progress toward being me somewhere else. I couldn't see the reality that my boss was no longer my friend. He didn't need me anymore, and we had grown apart. No judgment—just the reality.

Consider your judgments and your ego or desire when you're making decisions.

I Am a Seed

DAY 33

Be Here because Success Is Not Guaranteed

I WROTE MYSELF a check for $1 million and dated it June 19, 1993, then 1998, and then 2008. At no time could I cash that check. I worked hard to achieve this goal, and I came close in 1998—no debt, cash in the bank, great paying job, Porsche in the garage. Everything was going well, but that check was still there. I had to do something, and when it didn't happen, I started to blame others.

It was June 19, 2009, my birthday, I was fifty-two years old when I got the phone call from my lawyer. It was eight o'clock in the evening in Toronto, and I was with my son eating some great pizza.

My lawyer started: "There's no easy way to say this, but we lost, and big time. The judge also found against you, and you have to repay them $800,000 plus interest at 7 percent."

I lost everything.

The Mayans believe that you're reborn in your fifty-second year. Well, as it turns out, that was true for me.

We work so hard to make ends meet that we forget to be present, to enjoy the smallest of things, and to take time for ourselves. Then life happens. We get sick, or we lose our jobs, our savings, or a loved one. After that day, I couldn't cash any checks. I had no money left, but I was reborn with more value than I could ever have imagined: the value of presence.

Consider being here. Where are you present in your life today?

I Am a Seed

DAY 34

Your Change Is Difficult but Beautiful

NOTHING HURTS ME more than seeing someone I love struggle. Of course, my kids' struggles hit me the hardest. I feel incompetent and completely out of control. I know helping too much is worse than not helping, but not helping feels so wrong. I know they must fly, and I must be strong. I need to help just enough so they know I'm there, always. Even though I want to do more, I must resist because I know that on the other side of failure it's beautiful.

I've talked to so many parents, especially fathers, and it's heartbreaking to see them suffer. It's also heartbreaking when I see parents who can't let go—they feel a need to fix it. They feel a need to be stricter, more direct. I'm sad because the more they hold on, the less their loved ones will be able to function without them. I learned this the hard way; my job isn't to fix but to observe for dangers—to simply be there so that they can see me, feel my presence.

I know that if I judge you, you'll see it, and if I can't just love you and feel your struggles, you will not be able to find your path because my judgment is in the way and will blind you. I must be able to see the change in you that you do not see, and my job is to tell you that you're changing, and this difficult time will pass because you're changing your path.

Consider seeing the opportunity for change in the difficulties of life in those you love. List the things they love doing.

_____
_____
_____
_____
_____
_____
_____
_____
_____
_____
_____
_____
_____
_____
_____
_____
_____

I Am a Seed

DAY 35

Important Trophies Can't Be Shown but Can Be Seen

WHAT ARE YOUR real trophies? I asked myself. They were my diplomas, then a job, then salary increases, and then all my titles. I can't say these weren't important because at the time they were. I had nothing else. Then it was the people I knew and the moments with them, and then these trophies became my world. I name-dropped and saw others as less because I had more. These trophies defined who I was; they described my life, my accomplishments, and where I had been.

I met a wonderful lady named Heather Moyse. She won two Olympic gold medals and let me and others in the audience place one of them around our necks. I saw that the medal was a bit worn and scratched, and I wondered if she should have kept them in a safe place so they weren't destroyed.

She told me, "I had my moment, and that's in the past. Now, this is for you. You can feel and touch the gold medal and maybe, just maybe, get inspired for a better life."

That was the real trophy: the lesson she had learned. Once you achieve something, you have to share it with the world. That was her trophy—the one I didn't see. No wonder her eyes still shined.

I no longer have titles or hold on to the trophies. I share them because the real trophy is the mind shift—the things you feel by sharing what you've learned.

Consider letting go of the trophies and titles. What are some trophies you're holding on to?

I Am a Seed

DAY 36

Time Doesn't Change Things—You Do

TIME HEALS ALL wounds, as the saying goes. Well, it didn't help me until I started changing my habits, my mind, and my life. It wasn't until I took responsibility for the fact that I didn't have a name and no one knew what I stood for. No one knew the real me. They knew what I looked like and what I owned, where I lived, and maybe some trophies I had received, but did anyone truly know me?

How many people would you defend if they were accused? How many people would you go out of your way to help if they needed it? How many people would you lend money to without a contract?

When life hits you hard, you see who's left standing next to you pretty fast, and I was surprised at first and then took responsibility for it. It was my responsibility to stand for something. It was my responsibility to show my real self without the protection of my trophies. It was my responsibility to find what I stood for. This wasn't easy, and it took time, but as I wrote down my list of non negotiables that defined me, every new item on my daily list made me stronger and changed me.

Consider making a list of your nonnegotiables.

I Am a Seed

DAY 37

I Make Time; This Is the Secret to a Great Life

I WAS SO busy I hardly had time to drink my coffee; I took it on the run. Every minute, there was another emergency, another decision to make, one more call to place. My life was a list of to-dos with the only focus to get ahead. This worked, but I had no time and, to be honest, no life. I was alive, but I wasn't living; I was going from one sugar rush to the next, from one event to the next. Life went by fast.

I hardly remember it, but as I started taking notes of my thoughts and ideas during my twelve years as a board member of a large company, I realized that from one meeting to the next, every three months, the ideas were always the same ... The arguments were always the same ... My point of view was always the same.

My conclusion was that I was stuck in life—not moving anywhere—while the world changed around me. I stood still. I was living the same life year after year. Something had to change, and I realized it was me. I started to say no—no to the things that didn't feed my heart, no to the people who didn't fill my heart, and no to the places that didn't fill my heart. Suddenly, I had time to have a life—a different life every single day.

Consider saying no to one thing, place, or person who doesn't fill your heart.

I Am a Seed

DAY 38

I Want to Be Part of Something, Not Someone

I BELIEVED MY friend when he said we would all be rich. I believed him as I believed in my church pastor, my prime minister, and other business leaders. This was a mistake not because they fail but because unless humans stand for something bigger than themselves, they will always fall. We're designed to build communities. We're designed to leave this world a better place, and humans get lost behind the greed of the self and forget the community.

The dream of my friend was to be rich. This wasn't a dream to make anyone else rich but rather to *be* rich. I too wanted to be rich, so I fell for the lure—the dream that we, the community, would be rich. This wasn't a plan to build a better community; it was a plan to build a better army.

Most of our institutions are built on the fallacy of this promise and, I would argue, most relationships as well. Not leaving everything better for others but to build loyal followers who fall in love with you—or the idea of your wealth.

Love is actually based on accepting who you are and leaving everyone better, with understanding and compassion. Being part of something means that you're part of a family that shares those values; that family is your community, workplace, and city of residence.

I want to be the change I want to see in the world—a movement for conscious capitalism. This is a movement that understands how greed serves greed, but fairness feeds the world. I want to be what I fought so hard to protect. I want to be part of something—a positive change, a community, and a family. I don't want to be just part of someone. My plan is not to be rich or make my community rich; my dream is to allow everyone to discover for themselves who they are. My dream is not to build an army of followers but a movement of consciousness so that everyone can feed themselves.

Consider the movement or the destination you want to follow.

I Am a Seed

DAY 39

Changing Will Make You; Waiting Will Break You

WE LIVE IN a polarizing world; the more you don't change, the more you see what you believe. Social media works this way: what you like, share, and comment are all part of the algorithm. They just give you more of what you love.

This is the way the brain works as well—it's called confirmation bias. We surround ourselves with people who agree with us, we read the books that agree with us, and we go to places that agree with us. The big difference today is that it's never been easier to find our posse. This keeps us trapped and makes us angry at those who don't see what we see: our truth.

This is the big joke, I realized. We're all insane, and nothing will change until we change. The more we wait to change our minds or seek another truth, the angrier we get, and then, eventually, we break. Our brains can't take it, so we break or give up.

The alternative is to change—to look behind the mirror, to seek, and to wonder why we think the way we think, why we judge, and why we're not taking responsibility for our own lives and those in our communities.

Consider your confirmation bias.

I Am a Seed

DAY 40

Dreams Are Your Destinations; the Goals Are Your Plans

WE SPEND SO much time on our goals that we seem to forget our destination—our dreams. Maybe it's because our destination isn't clear. I know it wasn't clear for me, and to this day, it's still not clear. I know where I'm going, although I can't explain it because I can't see the future. I can only look back and realize the reasons I was doing what I did.

I don't spend time trying to figure out my future or trying to be happy. I simply do what makes me happy. I go with people who make me feel amazing, and I go places I call home. I set goals and use the goals to decide on what, where, and with whom I spend my time. An example would be that if I'm going out or making dinner, I think about how I can do something that would push my limits. I could invite a guest I've never invited but is intriguing to me. I could cook outside my comfort zone and offer it as a gift.

These are my goals. Instead of measuring the money I've saved, I could think of creative ways not to spend but still create a place, do something, or be with someone who lights up my heart. If I practice or teach yoga, I do it to meet other yogis and give to my community.

I think about how I want to be remembered and about the change I want to see in the world. I become that change.

Consider thinking about how you want to be remembered.

I Am a Seed

DAY 41

Allow Your Heart to Feel So Your Mind Gathers New Ideas

MY DAYTIME WORK is creating new software solutions for businesses—something I love to do. My focus has always been on innovation. How can I create something new to help people, to leave them a little better, to make them feel a little better every day? I've been in the technology field since I was a teenager building computers and software. I've been puzzled by the process of discovery and innovation ever since then.

I was always fascinated with my ideas and the fact that people I didn't know would copy my ideas. How is it that all my great ideas are copied so fast? As it turns out, it's really simple. People come up with the same ideas because we're subject to the same news, events, and pressures. This makes our brains react the same way. This is also true for investing; we all react to the same news and therefore all get the same ideas on which company to invest in.

I wanted to test this out, so I stopped reading the paper, listening to the radio, and watching the news on tv. Instead, I started to just observe. I observed how customers felt about products and services, how they were treated, and how products and services made me feel. In short, I listened to how my heart felt. Then I decided to buy stocks based on this feeling. My return over this five-year test was amazing. I more than doubled the standard market benchmarks. This was a solution toward more creative ideas.

Listening to your heart—or how it makes you feel when you get an idea—is the solution to creativity because not only will it set you apart, it will make you feel amazing. However, this shouldn't be confused with ego, which is more about how rich or successful you'll become. This is the same trap as before. You're not thinking about why this feels good; you're just feeding your ego.

Consider making decisions with observations from your heart. List the things that you do and how they make you feel.

_____
_____
_____
_____
_____
_____
_____
_____
_____
_____
_____
_____

I Am a Seed

DAY 42

To Be Less Reactive, Be More Reflective

WHY DO WE get angry at people we hardly know—our friends on Facebook, politicians, people on the radio, and, yes, those closest to us too? Why do some people get under our skin? We would prefer to just be angry and lash out instead of asking these questions. They don't know what they're doing and are responsible for this mess. Right?

Well, maybe ... Or instead, perhaps we should ask why we think that way. Where do these emotions come from—this anger-blame? What are these emotions? Why do we have them? Why am I angry at words? Who is responsible for this anger? Can I solve this another way? Can I ever be his friend again? Can I ever forgive? Can I ever forget? Can I ever just not be triggered?

Consider asking deeper questions about your emotions: Who? What? Where? Why? How?

Yves Doucet

I Am a Seed

DAY 43

Where You Aim Determines What You See

IF YOU'RE ABOUT to get married, you'll notice wedding dresses everywhere. When you buy a new Toyota Matrix, you're amazed at how many people drive your car, so much so that you can't find your car in the parking lot and some days even go to the wrong car.

This can also play against you because you only want to see what you're aiming for. If you believe in organic food, you'll also see it everywhere and will rejoice and talk about it and speak against nonorganic companies. They're now your enemies. They're not part of your tribe, so you must change them or demonize them. You get angry at them because they don't see what you see. Therefore, we see our loved ones with those eyes. We see what we want to see, and if they do not conform, we fight them.

It's interesting to understand how we vote; we believe that we choose willfully. In reality, we choose the one that looks like us and has a common belief. We vote against someone who doesn't believe in what we believe; therefore, the issues are so important and not the character or the values. Once we've decided to support that person, we have to defend our logical choice, and we demonize everyone who doesn't like our candidate. This person we've never met, this person whom before the election we wouldn't have considered a friend—we now defend him or her more than our closest friends.

Consider observing what you want to see.

I Am a Seed

DAY 44

I'm More Productive Now That I'm Less Reactive

WHEN WE OFFER our employees free coffee to give them energy, what are we really doing? Coffee is great to get going, but does it make you more productive?

I don't think so. I love coffee and have been a coffee lover for forty years, and there is good documentation on the health benefits for the brain, providing the building blocks it needs to get stronger. Coffee will also make you react to situations. These reactions are from your unconscious mind and will close the opportunity to observe and be present. Too much coffee will create more discussions but rarely more solutions because no one is listening, no one is moving, and no one is feeling the real discussion in the room. Too much coffee will cause more stress and, in the end, will make your meetings longer. More than likely, you'll actually require another meeting to resolve the same issue. Being present for your meetings is key to being more productive. If you're not present, you can't listen with attention without reacting. You're not productive because reacting leads to miscommunication and, therefore, stress.

During a conference, the organizers who supplied the food, decided that we should have no coffee for seven days. I drink four shots of espresso daily. This was ridiculous, so I asked why.

"We ask that you don't consume alcohol, drugs, or coffee, and that you don't take notes," he replied.

Now I was really confused. How would I learn? How would I remember?

He simply said, "We want you to be here."

I thought about this for two days, and after the third day, I got it. We need to take coffee and notes to remember logically, but if we can remember emotionally, it will stay with us forever. Being present allows you to feel and see, and that is more powerful than coffee.

To be present and not reactive requires a disciplined mind—a mind that can recognize the difference between its ego talking and the need for words. I now drink less coffee, exercise every hour, and meditate daily to focus on productivity.

Consider switching coffee with five minutes of exercise. Then, journal about the energy and your mood, as well as ideas and discoveries.

I Am a Seed

DAY 45

No One Is Perfect, Yet We Seek It; Everyone Is Unique, Yet We Hide It

I'VE WON A lot of trophies—Entrepreneur of the Year and Innovator of the Year to name a few. But did these help me in my darkest hours? No, they didn't. They didn't help because they weren't me; they were the suit I was wearing as a disguise and as a pretense to be someone I wasn't. I hid behind these trophies, and they appealed to my ego and my self-preservation.

I didn't have to work at being a better me. All I had to do was win the trophies so everyone would admire me for my accomplishments. Then I would—I could—help the world be better. So, when I got hit with life, I couldn't bring these trophies to court and show the judge what I had done—what I had accomplished—because he was looking at who I was, not what I did. I wasn't my father either, and I wasn't my family; I was who I was.

When we're faced with our darkest hours, we're faced with who we are: all the regrets, all the mistakes, and all the wrongs we've done. There is no hiding these because *you are your own judge*. It may help you to do more, but this will be temporary because the judgments you make on others are the ones you make on yourself.

At that moment, I decided to refuse nominations for trophies and refuse all accolades that are not only self-serving but worse, give you a false sense of the self.

I saw my trigger (a trigger is a person who makes you remember a past emotion) win an award yesterday, and I thought I had put this behind me, but it came to get me. I was angry at the world.

This is what's wrong with the world, I told myself. *We place people who are good at making money on a pedestal without regard for their communities.* I was angry because I wanted to change the world. Then I realized that to believe that I could change the world was the same thing. I believed I was worth more than others and was just looking for another trophy. "Be the change you want to see in the world." I then remembered: If I truly wanted to live by these words of fairness, then I would have to realize that I had to *be* that change. Now, that made me feel amazing and got my heart in the right place.

Consider being the change you want to see in the world. What do you stand against, or what are your triggers? Can you find the positive opposite and be that change?

_____
_____
_____
_____
_____
_____
_____

I Am a Seed

DAY 46

We May Ask for Your Time, but We Crave Your Energy, Your Attention, and Your Presence

I WAS HAVING a difficult discussion with a good friend, and she was telling me how right she was. She was sharing her opinion about a situation and her plan to take care of it. So I intervened and proceeded to tell her my thoughts on the subject—that maybe she wasn't open to listening, and her ego was talking.

She stopped me and said, "I don't want to listen to you right now. I want you to listen to me."

So I shut up but found my ego bouncing on what she asked me to do. Could I simply listen? It was difficult. What was my role then? It felt like an empty discussion. I had a hard time with my own ego and couldn't just listen. All I could do was oscillate between my ego, trying to be perfect, and helping, even though her demands were clear: "I just want you to listen."

Can I be present? No, I couldn't just be present and listen. I felt like she was stealing my energy, but truly, it was my ego stealing my energy. I wanted to be right. I wanted to tell her that her ego wasn't going to let her listen.

She wanted my attention, my energy, and my presence, and I was so busy trying to be right that I couldn't and didn't have any energy left for her. Later at the office, the same thing happened with a coworker. I started to let my ego speak instead of just listening, and that discussion went nowhere. It drained me as well. I stopped myself again and observed how I felt: I was on empty again.

I have a hard time—maybe it's a man thing—always having the need to fix things instead of simply being there and just listening. When do we need to say something? I've had the opportunity to observe Eckhart Tolle up close. He didn't say one word as people around him were asking him questions. He simply listened as they themselves answered their own questions. He simply looked and observed. Maybe part of the solution was fewer words—just fewer words and more observation.

First, observe my ego and then the person in front of me. Don't observe in judgment—that would be ego rather than curiosity in simply seeing the human in front of me. *How would that look?* I asked myself.

I saw the love, the smile, the human just trying to be a human. I saw the pain and the complexity of life, and I enjoyed the conversation. More importantly, I didn't feel empty; I felt energized. That to me was a trophy—a prize to take home. It felt better than trying to fix or solve the problem. I felt better about being present rather than being right.

I Am a Seed

Consider just listening to the next conversation. Consider the feeling of being present. Can you write about your difficulty to listen?

Yves Doucet

DAY 47

Don't Let Ego Drive Your Dreams; Let Purpose Make Them a Reality

WE ALL HAVE those dreams—I had them. It looked like something out of the *Ironman* movies, where I would use technology to do good; all I needed was to become great at developing it. Then I could do it—then I could give back to the community. This is not unlike our dream of becoming rich. I would divide the money up with those I love, becoming the judge of that love. Then if I had lots, I would become a philanthropist. In the meantime, I would give spare change to the homeless man as I walk by, rushing in to make this dream happen.

This dream, as it turns out, is not mine; it's not even real. It's a fabrication—a figment of the creative mind. This is such an appealing dream that we spend money to follow it. We dream of the perfect love or the perfect relationship. Again, they're not our dreams because they don't exist; they're someone else's life or dream. So we let our ego drive us to our dreams without considering that it's not even our dream. But we want it so much that we're willing to do anything to get it; our ego and our pride are running our lives.

Once I stopped running, I started to ask myself: What drives me deeper than anything to have that dream? Why do I believe in that dream that is not mine? What is my why? The simple exercise of writing in two columns, first the stories that marked my life as a child and second the emotions I felt at the time, provided me some insight into what I loved to do. Inside these stories was my true self, without the ego.

These stories built my foundation to becoming an inventor to make this world a better place, but I didn't need to become *Ironman*. I needed to figure out the answer to the question: What is innovation? Innovation is community, and innovation grows in community. I had it backward—I didn't need to be an inventor to serve. I had to build a community. I had to serve first and then innovate.

Consider your childhood dreams.

_____
_____
_____
_____
_____
_____
_____
_____
_____
_____
_____
_____

I Am a Seed

DAY 48

Life Is Impossible without Love; Love What You Do, and Love Who You Are

I'VE BEEN LUCKY in that most jobs I've had, I loved. I enjoyed the challenge and for the most part fell into the next job … The jobs seemed to just find me. I got lost in my work, and when asked if I was happy, I would answer yes with pride, actually. That should've been my first warning, as pride is not happiness, but I didn't know what I didn't know. Maybe there was some peace in not knowing—anyone can surely accept that—because although I enjoyed and loved my work, the sense of accomplishment was the drive, and it blinded me to the deeper truth: I didn't love myself. That was a deep shock that I uncovered too late in life. Call it a midlife crisis, one where you start to question everything, but I was lucky because I had nothing left. So the questions I asked myself weren't about my trophies but about who I was.

Did I love myself enough to be alone but not lonely? Did I love myself enough to be with someone but still be myself? Did I love myself enough to follow the things I needed to do in life, even though others—my friends, my family—didn't like them? Could I love myself enough to be judged? Well no, that took time and patience, like peeling an onion—every little layer was emotional until I found myself closer to the middle.

Can I love myself enough to do without the need to justify? Almost.

Consider having the courage to do what you love to do. What or who stands in your way?

_____

_____

_____

_____

_____

_____

_____

_____

_____

_____

_____

_____

_____

_____

_____

I Am a Seed

DAY 49

If You Don't Take a Break, You Will Break

I WAS RUNNING two shifts of engineers; we had a deadline. I was running the teams 24/7. I remember getting home to take a shower and have breakfast with my kids only to leave again until later that night. This went on for a year, and then before we could break, we started another project, this time flying across the world every second week. I enjoyed a vacation in which I stayed active and drank too much; we laughed and had a good time, but I came back more tired than before I left. I was young, and I could take it. My job was a necessity—my job defined me.

What I learned later was that muscles need rest to grow. If all you do is train at the gym, you're only ripping your muscles and not giving them enough time to grow more powerful, so they just get weaker. Growth happens in the state of rest. Thinking about this made sense. The rebuilding happens during peacetime, when you're asleep and take the time needed to feed those muscles.

This wasn't new to Olympians, but it was new to me. What blew me away was that this is also true for the mind. It needs to rest, and rest is not a vacation. It's actually not doing much. Just walking in the woods or on the beach. This is not only important but a necessity; if you don't rest your brain, much like a permanent physical injury, you will get a permanent mental injury. I discovered daily meditation, massages, yoga, and time alone.

Consider a mind vacation. Describe a perfect mental holiday.

_____
_____
_____
_____
_____
_____
_____
_____
_____
_____
_____
_____
_____
_____
_____
_____
_____
_____

I Am a Seed

DAY 50

The Only Way to Escape Is to Change Your Mind

WE ESCAPE OUR reality with entertainment, motivational speakers, books, and all sorts of other ways. We all have our things—I've been there. I've spent well over three hundred hours on self-help and motivational speeches. I've read more than two hundred books on business innovation and self-help alone. Americans spend close to eight hours a day watching television to find a solution and try to escape this madness. We take holidays with organized tours or stay in resorts to escape the world.

It's the reason motivational speakers can make so much money for one hour—some more than $100,000 an hour. These are the same reasons that resorts and television are so lucrative.

Nothing changes until you change your mind. The emotional attachment we have to our stories will always win over logic. The emotional memory is more powerful because it has all the emotions, not just one. We feel, smell, see, hear, and sometimes taste it, and all of these are registered into our systems as memories. The logic has no chance. So we go back and listen and learn again until we become discouraged. It's why we give up on diets and the gym—the emotional memory is more powerful than the reasons we need to lose weight.

The secret, as it turns out, is simple: Ask yourself deep questions about your behaviors and your feelings. Exercise and then sit in silence. And then ask yourself serious questions. You can also ask others serious questions about your behavior or listen to constructive criticism. Just remember you're not your actions or decisions; these were just memories that guided you. They've been programmed with emotions, and only a reprogramming with emotion will change your behavior. These emotional memories are in your subconscious mind; just like with walking, they happen and are triggered without your knowledge. They're your learned behaviors and can only be changed by new emotional memories.

Consider changing your mind. Consider remembering the good things from a bad experience.

I Am a Seed

DAY 51

Leadership Is Not About Taking It Personally but Making It Personal

WE ARE ALL leaders when given the chance. Nando Parades taught me this life lesson; he was one of the survivors of the plane crash in the Andes. His book, *Miracle in the Andes*, describes the events of his survival.

Each time a leader dies, another one takes his place. We all have the ability to be leaders. *Leader* is not a title we give ourselves. It's a title given to us. We don't become leaders; people chose to follow us. We get confused and believe it's only the people who are successful or who win the fight who can be leaders and we must follow them.

The biggest lesson I learned about leadership is that it's personal. Great leaders make things personal; they give us hope and allow us to keep moving forward in the belief of their hope—that very personal hope. We're drawn to them not because they say the words but because they express their beliefs in everything they do. They may not have a plan, but they have a dream; they may not be rich, but they give with their presence. They're personal.

When they fail or are attacked—and they are—they don't blame or take it personally. They forgive and continue the journey. They take and make their journeys personal.

Consider that you must choose who you follow. List the people you hold dear and the reasons why.

_____
_____
_____
_____
_____
_____
_____
_____
_____
_____
_____
_____
_____
_____
_____
_____
_____
_____
_____

I Am a Seed

DAY 52

The Kinder I Get, the Stronger I Become

SOCIETY HAS A way of making you feel guilty if you don't give money to charity. It's become the default way for some to pretend to be kind. Easy to give $1 million if you have $200 million; easy to give old clothes if you have new ones. It's always harder to be kind without any intention. Becca Schofield understood this sleight of hand: To really get stronger and not feed the ego, you must be kind without intent.

This means being kind in silence to people who hurt you. An act of kindness without getting credit is a pure muscle builder. The simplest acts—the ones that don't make the papers, the ones that come with a feeling of peace and calm, the ones without witnesses—strengthen you. It can be as simple as a smile, leaving everything and everyone better.

Don't get me wrong—I applaud all those who give their time and money to protect our communities; however, this will not build your inner strength. To build inner strength it must be given without an ulterior motive or intent.

We understand that if our communities don't see us as kind, we may be left out of them. This draw to being kind is a survival instinct more powerful than we can ever imagine. The power of kindness is explained in the book *The Secret* by Rhonda Byrne and has been known for thousands of years. Every religion has a tenet of kindness, but what no one has explained yet is that the power of kindness works to provide you with a sense of belonging. That sense of belonging creates a positive effect on your brain and makes you open your eyes to the possibilities of your life—of evolution. However, if you give to the church to pay for a miracle, nothing will happen because it doesn't work that way. If you give without intent and become open to the possibilities, then you'll see the benefits of kindness.

Consider giving without intent. How did you feel?

I Am a Seed

DAY 53

"I'm Not Enough" Is Not a Fact; It's a Reason—Don't Make It Yours

HAVE YOU EVER noticed the most creative people are the ones who had to deal with big trauma in their lives? Rejection, humiliation, abuse, and atrocities. These people are the deep thinkers, the artists who shake the world and, in some cases, reinvent it. They're the oddballs, the rejected, and the abandoned. They're also the ones who dug deep inside and looked at their narrative, their voices inside, to reinvent themselves. They had to deal with blaming others—usually their parents—only to realize it was just a narrative, a story they told themselves when they were young to protect themselves against evil.

This was important when you were a child because it's stories like these that are told from one generation to another. That's why behaviors run in the family. They had to deal with this to protect the future generations, but as adults, we don't realize that we're programmed. These leaders had to reprogram their brains so they could realize the danger is not there and can't hurt them.

Here's the big joke: We all have these stories, but we don't know them. When everything is going great (like it was in my life), we think there's nothing wrong. The stories will turn out, maybe as a life trauma, broken relationships, or poor health, but by then it may be too late. You can't fix your narrative because you're stuck in a downward spiral.

Consider that your mistakes are just a narrative, a story. Can you write your mistakes and then write "So What" next to each one?

I Am a Seed

DAY 54

Don't Focus on Team Building; Focus on Habits of Empathy

MY TEAM AT Dovico.com and I are all from this small place called Moncton, New Brunswick, yet we built a product that took the world by storm. We beat the biggest companies with billions of dollars in revenues—giants in the industry compared to our small size. We did amazing things. The question, however, is what is special about this city? Is Moncton the epicenter of the brightest people in the world, and did we achieve these projects because we had the best players in the world?

The team is a powerful catalyst for innovation and creativity, but the team must be like a family and a community.

We never focus on team building. We focus on listening, observing, and having empathy. We all win together, and we all lose together. We celebrate each other. We celebrate not the wins but the moments. We laugh, and we cherish the memories. This creates an innovative environment. We don't succeed because we have the skills or the determination or even the opportunities. We succeed because we have a community that is open to the possibilities. Our community has the courage to follow what they love to do, and they believe the community will eventually prosper.

Consider your team as your community for ideas and creativity. Write about the discovery of new ideas or delivering with your community (family, friends or work).

I Am a Seed

DAY 55

It Feels Like a Life When You Are Present

"CAN YOU COME and help your grandson?" my wife asked with panic in her voice.

Then I heard it. He was crying. He was curled up in a ball and crying uncontrollably.

"He's upset because he can't finish his project," my wife told me as she turned to him and said, "Just breathe. Just breathe."

Of course, there was no danger, but for him, the fear was real, and my heart sank as I just observed—oh, how I love him so much. I saw the pain in his face as the tears rolled down his cheeks, but I said nothing, I simply observed and focused on my breath. My ego wanted to help, wanted to say something, but I simply focused on what I saw, what I felt, and my breathing. Soon he started to calm down, and as he wiped his tears, he took a long, deep breath. My face smiled. He was coming out. I could see him, and he could see me.

"I have to have three minutes for my presentation, and I only have two. I don't know what else to say to fill that missing minute," he explained.

I said nothing and observed. I saw how fast he was working in PowerPoint and said, "Oh my goodness, you're super-fast!" I wanted to ask so many questions, and then I saw the title of his presentation: "My Bucket List."

"Have you considered the Roman Colosseum?" I went on my iPad and brought up some pictures. "This is the biggest colosseum in the world. It holds eighty thousand people, it's five times bigger than the one we have here, and it was built two thousand years ago. They had lions and gladiators there!" I didn't have to say anything else—he had already placed it in his presentation. Within fifteen minutes, we were done.

As he cleaned up his presentation, he asked me, "What did you mean when you said I was fast on PowerPoint?"

I said nothing. He continued talking about why, and then he went into why he was late. He first began blaming the teachers, and then saying he was anxious because he was afraid that I would come up and tell him to go to bed as it was now nine thirty at night. That was the anxiety—he was afraid of the future and what was coming. I was the cause of his anxiety, so how could I have fixed it with words of judgment? Then he said, "I guess I could have started earlier." He looked at me. We started laughing uncontrollably.

You can't ask someone to be present. You must be present. This was a moment I won't forget; it was a moment when I was a good grandad, when I was a good dad, when I was enough. If

I Am a Seed

I've achieved nothing else in my life, that moment is the one I'll remember because of how it made me feel.

Consider your real intention with your words. Can you write about when you said too much?

_____
_____
_____
_____
_____
_____
_____
_____
_____
_____
_____
_____
_____
_____
_____
_____
_____
_____
_____
_____
_____
_____
_____

Yves Doucet

DAY 56

Growth Doesn't Happen When You're Right; It Happens When You're Open

THE FIRST PART of my life I was right, and it took fifty-two years to realize that although I had done some stuff, I had not evolved. I had achieved big things, seen many exotic places, and checked so many things off my list. I was on my way to freedom at fifty-five, which I believed was my dream.

As it turned out, it wasn't retirement; retirement was invented by the Germans in the early 1900s in order to get the older generation to give way to young workers. Because there weren't enough jobs to go around, they made it mandatory to retire at sixty-five years old with benefits extended to the end of their lives. The average life expectancy was sixty-eight at the time, so not a very big benefit.

The insurance companies in the 1970s realized the potential for a product called Freedom 55, and they exploited the tired workers with visions of vacations, skiing, and fishing. "This could be you;

this is the dream!" It was the freedom to do what you want to do at the end of your life—to just enjoy life. Nothing wrong with that, right? Well, maybe just a few things.

Now that life expectancy is eight-six years old—and according to most experts on the subject, we're not meant to do nothing—we're realizing that we're meant to do useful work. We're designed to use our muscles and our brains to contribute. If we don't use our brains, they start to decay. I was wrong about life, working, what work is, the purpose of work, and the meaning of life. I had been programed with someone else's dream.

Was this true for most things? I questioned everything. Had I opened Pandora's box? Was I just seeing the reality that was projected on Plato's wall? As it turned out, that's exactly what the brain does to protect and focus your choices. Your brain executes your beliefs to protect you. Everything you believe to be right feeds the same narrative, and you live the same day repeatedly. You can't learn if you're right, you can't listen if you're right, and you can't live if you're right.

Consider that you are wrong. Write down your belief and why you could be wrong.

_____

_____

_____

_____

_____

_____

_____

I Am a Seed

DAY 57

Make Excuses or Be Inspired by the Possibilities

I WAS A master of excuses but didn't realize they were excuses. I just believed they were logical. That's what logic is—excuses or reasons, why we think what we think and why we behave the way we behave. We see this in others—how they can't see their destructive behaviors and how their reasons don't make sense. I didn't see this before. I had to understand the concept of differences in worldviews or the narrative behind Plato's wall. I believed that because I could think it meant I was in control of my life, but in reality, my thoughts controlled me. The real question is: Why are you thinking what you're thinking? Start with that question, not why are you right but, rather, why you *need* to be right.

I was a very successful man who decided to risk everything he had to prove a point. This was seen by my friends as insanity. According to Albert Einstein, insanity is doing the same thing over and over again and expecting different results. But I didn't know I was insane. I was stuck in my narrative, my world, and my reasons and didn't see that it was the voices in my own head that were making the choices.

Once you know the truth about your reasons—the real reasons—you can then be open to the possibilities. The reasons are why doors are closing, the reasons are why you don't act, and the reasons are why you can't see your possibilities.

Consider that behind your logic are only reasons and excuses. Write down the reasons why you *need* to be right.

_____
_____
_____
_____
_____
_____
_____
_____
_____
_____
_____
_____
_____
_____
_____
_____
_____

I Am a Seed

DAY 58

What You Judge, You Are; What You See, You Become

ASK ONE HUNDRED people to close their eyes and raise their hands if they believe this question to be true: "Do you believe that you're a better driver than most people?" About 80 percent would say yes. This is impossible because everyone can't be a better driver than the other person, but yet we believe we are. We judge other people for speeding a little more than us, for cutting us off, for texting, and for driving while talking on the phone.

We're who we choose to judge. That's why life gives us those examples, not to judge them but to show us who we are. The more we judge, the more we're like the ones we're judging.

So I stopped judging bad drivers and started to see the people walking in the rain. I let them cross. I saw the motorcycle in front and imagined him having a flat tire. I gave him more room. Suddenly, no one was on my bumper, and no one was cutting me off. Everyone, well, okay, 80 percent were better drivers than me.

Consider judgment to be a reflection. Where are you judging?

I Am a Seed

DAY 59

You're No Longer Restricted to Where You Are, Only by *What* You Are

I'M REALLY SURPRISED and amazed at the power of social media. It affects our moods, our actions, and our lives. The things we consume make us who we are. This is true for food, information, consumption, and clothing. It's well recognized that you will become your closest friends. It's simple, really. You'll modify your habits to their habits, and soon you'll be in the same shape, have the same income, and lead the same lives. This is why we move into certain neighborhoods.

This is also true of social media, so some will decide to turn it off because it's too negative. But, here's the catch: social media engines only feeds you what it believes you want, so look at what it feeds you and change what you like, share, and post. Pretty soon, you'll have new friends from all over the world simply because of what you see, you are.

Consider that everything leaves an impression that leads to your best life. Write about what you share and like and post on social media or in a conversation.

I Am a Seed

DAY 60

Opportunity Is Everywhere Once You're Balanced

I LEARNED A long time ago that to have a beautiful lawn, you don't need to feed it the nutrients that sell for twenty dollars a bag. That's what the store wants you to buy; however, the nutrients have no effect if the soil is not PH balanced. To get it balanced, you typically have to spread lime, which costs about five dollars a bag (which is also twice the size of the expensive nutrients). But that's not what we buy. We want the food because we want results right away.

This is the same for the food we eat. If we're stressed, we're not feeding our bodies because in stress mode we're not balanced, and food has very little effect. You need to balance your body first in order to be ready to receive the food. The body is like this because if you're in a fight-or-flight state, running from the bear, the last thing you want to be doing is eating, peeing, or stopping to tie your shoes. Your body is geared to run or fight, not eat or digest.

Similarly, if your ego is taking over the conversation or if fear or anxiety is taking over the conversation, the body gets ready to run or fight. It can't hear and can't see anything else other than the danger in front of it. You're not balanced and can't see the opportunities. In order to feed your mind the right thing, you must breathe through the nose—long, deep breaths so that it tells your nervous system there's no danger, and you have nothing to fear. It balances your mind, so you can see the opportunities.

Consider doing a balancing exercise before eating. Can you balance on one foot and inhale for four seconds, hold for four seconds, and then exhale for eight seconds? Can you repeat this five times before you eat? Write about how this makes you feel.

I Am a Seed

DAY 61

I'm Not Who I Want To Be. Will You Love Me Anyway?

I USED TO get mad at team members, my friends, and my family. Why didn't they listen to me? Now I laugh at this statement. I needed to get over myself. Who do I think I am to tell them about their paths? Worse, I was living vicariously through them, and I didn't like my performance in them.

The best coaches don't show you the way because they don't know your path. Your path is yours. The best coaches will give you the tools to help you discover your path. they'll allow you to fail, to learn, and to be human. When you do fail, they'll sit with you, be present for you, and breathe with you. The best coaches will see the pain, the frustration, and the love in you. The best coaches will see love in struggles because in your presence is the power to help find the path.

My mom was a master at this. She was once and still is a master coach. When we were in difficulty, stressed, or depressed, she would sit in silence next to us. Her silence was powerful and energetic. I felt loved with no judgment—I had hope. Love and hope were all I needed to get up. Even in my darkest hour, I could feel her, but she wasn't there; she didn't call me. When I went to see her, she would just observe me. She took my pain and my bad energy and replaced it with love and hope. She loves me without judgment, and she loves me as I am. I slowly got up and started again. More than anything, unconditional love saved my life.

Consider love as a guide. Write about the moments when you felt that your love was unconditional.

I Am a Seed

DAY 62

You Can't Give What You Don't Have; Practice Happiness

IF YOU ASK most parents what they want the most, they will say, "For my kids to be happy." Nothing, and I mean nothing, will bring you to your knees faster than seeing your child struggle, in pain, sad, or depressed. We want to dive in and fix it, take care of it, so they can be happy. Here's a shocker: You can't give what you don't have, and the only way to fix anything is to fix yourself. Life is hard, and we will all die. We're born, and we die, but we don't all *live*. What we do in between is the important stuff.

We try to work hard to earn money to buy the best things for our loved ones, so they can be comfortable and happy. We do this because if we don't have any money, we can't give it to them, so what is the purpose of money? To make us happy? Are we really working at being happy? We think that the secret to happiness is to work hard, become successful, and then be happy. But life doesn't work that way. Millions work hard but are never successful and therefore never happy; they then live in regret or in sickness. The better formula is be happy at what you do, work hard, and then be successful. You can then give what you have—happiness.

Every morning I pay myself first. I invest in making me happy; I do things that I move my heart.

Consider being happy. What will I do tomorrow that makes me happy? List in detail what, where, and with whom.

I Am a Seed

DAY 63

Don't Make Me Responsible For Your Happiness; It's Yours to Keep

I GET CONFUSED as a man. It seems that my role is to provide for my family. This is now being questioned. It seems that my role is to protect, but this too is being questioned. Is my role to be strong? Most would question that as well. Can you understand my confusion? Am I responsible for your happiness? We're confused because we're listening to two voices: one from the ego and the other from the heart.

Recently, I attended a conference of motivational speakers where some talked about their paths to overcoming tragedy in their lives. It felt empowering but resolved nothing in me because the message was intended to empower them. Their message was, "I was down, but I overcame." It left me with unsolved questions simply because the message that was given had mixed directions. The first began with: this is me—abused, depressed, and contemplating dark thoughts. This is a message of kindness and tenderness and brings us in close, so we feel. Then the message changed to: I survived and beat the odds. I'm successful. This is a message of ego, and it really mixed me up. How can this be? What and who am I?

Of course, we want to see and applaud the rise from nothing—this is the hero's journey. But the real hero then becomes of service. The real hero sees that she could not do this alone. The real hero understands her ego and the effect it has. The real hero understands that her newfound power must serve her community, and she must leave us with a message of service, not of ego for our hearts to be in the right place.

I now understand that as a human I'm not responsible for anyone else's happiness. As a dad, I can't make my children happy. As an employer, I can't be responsible for the path of my employees. I can only be responsible for my happiness and my path. I've come to realize that I have to let you be responsible for your path and your happiness. I can't make you work hard at being happy without ego and with kindness and generosity. This is the biggest responsibility I have: to let you be responsible.

Consider that it's not your responsibility to make others happy. Where are you trying to buy the happiness of others?

I Am a Seed

DAY 64

I Respect You, So I'll Let You Choose Your Path

GREAT LEADERS DON'T guide or coach or even dictate. They observe and empower you with the possibility to consider the courage to go down your path just a little farther. Great leaders look for the opportunities. They look for the beauty and sparkle in the eye. They observe your emotions and see the pain, and they just point you the way you know deep inside you that you should go. Great leaders look at your heart.

This is one of the most difficult things to do as a parent, a friend, and a boss. I want so much to tell, to teach, and to direct with my wisdom—well, maybe that's what I believe. No one wants to be told what to do. Everyone wants to discover what to do—to have it fall into their laps. I remember my son and I trying to figure this out as he changed from a boy into a man. I started to give him choices until I could see what moved him and what gave him self-esteem. He was able to discover his love of food and entertainment—nothing could stop him from creating memorable events. To this day, nothing can stop him. He loves making people smile and the surprise on others' faces when he presents something unexpected. I love him so much that it hurt not to help him, but he wanted to do it on his own. It was going to be his path, and if that meant him not agreeing with me, so be it. I just had to love and observe. My love for him helped me discover my son and see his unique path.

Consider that your path is yours and yours alone. Can you see the love in what your loved ones are doing? Can you write about it?

I Am a Seed

Yves Doucet

DAY 65

Our Biggest Mistake Is That We Give Our Happiness Away

I'VE GONE ON holiday to some amazing places, and sometimes I'm asked to share my experiences. I'm happy to; however, this feels empty and void of the happiness—it's like I'm giving my happiness away. It seems the more I talk about my trips, the places I have seen, the food I've tasted, or the beauty of the architecture or beaches, the more I feel I must go back to those places. It becomes an addiction to the place and not to the moment. It feeds my ego, not my heart. A feeling of emptiness overcomes me. I've come to understand that it's because the ego is talking, and its job is to destroy my happiness—to destroy the feeling of joy.

The more I talk about what I've done, the more the ego makes me crave for more and the more I feel lonely or lost without the next adventure. The ego is good at its job, and we give our happiness away by feeding it.

When I returned from my trip to Mexico—a beautiful resort where I took my yoga teacher training—I was tempted to tell everyone about the beaches and the food and the resort. I did, but then I stopped because it didn't feel right. Instead, I started talking about my feelings about the people I met. I was just sharing the moments that changed my life and touched me. I was giving them a gift of love, without intent. When you lead with love, you become present, and you observe, and you change.

During my sharing, an idea came to me. I was privileged to be able to have such experiences. Why not create a program at work that would allow everyone to have the courage to find themselves and have life-changing experiences? I named the program Courage. The intention was the name, the intention was more important than the rules.

The rules were simple. Every two years everyone could receive up to $3,000 to explore their inner selves. This blew me away because now it wasn't my ego talking; it was my heart, and it was giving to and building a community. My experience meant so much more because I was excited to hear and see the experiences of others in my community. I can't wait to see what happens next. I'm sure it will be unexpected and beautiful.

Consider sharing how you feel as a gift. Write about the feeling of the experience and how it affected your life. Do you now feel something different?

_____
_____
_____
_____
_____
_____
_____
_____

I Am a Seed

DAY 66

I'm Just as Blind as Yesterday, but Today I Know It

MY FRIEND JAMES once took a ten-day silent retreat. Afterward, he asked his master, "Am I awakened? I feel that I see life differently now."

"Not yet," replied the master.

So James decided to do a thirty-day retreat at which point he asked the master the same question. He was now so sure because his journey of thirty days was so powerful and so incredibly insightful.

"Not yet," replied the master.

Our minds play tricks on us; they make us believe we know the path, that we can see the future, and that we're the masters of our domains. Life, however, has a different idea. It's there to constantly challenge our being so that the path to the truth is always changing and we must just be open to the change. This has never been so true as today with technology always changing, with our markets always changing, and with our relationships always in flux. We can never truly be a master and never truly be awakened to see everything.

Our only solution is presence: to observe and see that this is the only truth. The past doesn't exist. Neither does the future. Think about that for a moment. The only thing that exists is here, now.

Steve Jobs once said: "If this was the last day of your life, would you do what you are going to do today? This is a question that you must write in your journal every day. If the answer is 'no' for too many days in a row, consider changing something, consider learning something new."

Consider being a student today and answer this question: "If this was the last day of my life, would I do what I am about to do today?"

_____
_____
_____
_____
_____
_____
_____
_____
_____
_____
_____
_____
_____

I Am a Seed

MY LAST MESSAGE

What if this was the last day of my life? What if this was the last message I had to share? What if this was my last breath? What would I use my last words to say? This question was asked by my good friend Karen after she had read the book, and it took me deeper into my purpose. Life is less about hoping to get everything you want so you can be happy but rather accepting yourself and finding hope within. This question left me thinking about my time in the hospital with my dad and the words we shared. He did get better, and I was relieved that he could finally go home. I then asked myself, *What would I say with my last breath?*

"Ask and you shall receive." I grew up with this in mind but never quite understood how it worked. If I ask for a new car, why didn't I receive it? If I asked for someone to heal, why didn't they heal? To be sure, I've been a bit confused by this statement. What if the interpretation is wrong? What if this meant I should ask questions about who I am? The most important thing I want to leave with you is this:

If you ask questions about your behavior, how it made you feel will give you the answer, which will lead to a new you, a new hope, and a new life. Ask the right question, and you'll receive the answer. You *are* everything you need to be. You *are* everything you want to be.

MY LAST RECOMMENDATION

If you're like me, you probably read the book and didn't spend any time writing. Start again, but this time do one story a day and write something—one phrase, one paragraph, or one page. It doesn't matter what you write. What matters is that you write. If the story doesn't resonate with you, it's okay. Consider one word, maybe the first one you see on the page, and write a phrase about that word. Consider that this habit will change your life.

Thank you for your time and consideration.

Love you,
Yves

BOOK RECOMMENDATIONS

Man's Search for Meaning by Viktor Frankl

Braving the Wilderness by Brené Brown

Tears to Triumph by Marianne Williamson

Redefining 'Realistic' by Heather Moyse

Flow by Mihaly Csikszentmihalyi

The Untethered Soul by Michael A. Singer

The Four Agreements by Miguel Ruiz

Evolve Your Brain by Joe Dispenza

The Wealthy Barber by David Chilton

Buffett by Roger Lowenstein

The Rise of Superman by Steven Kotler

The Bible

A Course in Miracles by Dr. Helen Schucman

The Power of Habit by Charles Duhigg

Find Your Why by Simon Sinek

Ego Is the Enemy by Ryan Holiday

The Power of Now by Eckhart Tolle

Talent is Overrated by Geoff Colvin

Miracles in the Andes by Nando Parrado

The Ripple Effect by Greg Wells

The Leader Who Had No *Title* by Robin Sharma

DEDICATION

I dedicate this book to my coaches. They're my foundation and my hope. There's always a risk in offending those I haven't mentioned, but just because they're not on the list, it doesn't lessen the love and importance in my life. However, I would be remiss if I did not list those who appeared most in my life through my journey during the last eight years.

Suzelle Doucet, my financial and minimalist coach.

A few times a year, I go visit my daughter at her home, where she has three knives, three forks, etc. She has no car and owns no house, yet she's financially independent. She's managed to not only save money but has accumulated enough that she could stop working and live comfortably. I go visit her to learn how to simplify my life and how to save money and time. She's the model example of a better, simpler life.

Luc Doucet, my creative coach

I spend as much time as I can with Luc. I go to every event he produces. They're creative and new every single time. He continues to push the limits of what is a restaurant, what is the intent of eating, and what makes a community. The inspiration for the creative process that keeps me pushing my limits.

Dianne Doucet, my mood coach

My wife, Dianne, is a master at setting the mood for family events—every single detail is taken into consideration. Family, of course, is the reason we're here. It's our most precious community. The environment will push the intent of the event to new levels. Much like Steve Jobs understood the quality of the design, my wife understands the impact of every detail of the family home. I'm always amazed at the change in people's faces as soon as they walk in the door. She's the example of family gathering and the essence of environment.

Rheal LeBlanc, my business coach

Rheal has been in business his entire life and has learned the importance of a person's word and integrity. He can almost predict the outcome of the relationship and has proven me wrong on more than one occasion. He's a master at human behavior and how it affects the decisions we make; before I make a decision, I ask Rheal.

Jeannita LeBlanc, my family coach

Every year we meet for Christmas at her home, and every year—except for this one because she had heart surgery—Jeannita prepares her home to receive the whole family. Every year she hangs the stockings filled with gifts. With considerable care, she prepares ten to fifteen gifts in each stocking, each gift wrapped for the whole family, which now numbers twenty-eight. At eighty-seven years old, Jeannita understands the value of family and the importance of each member feeling welcomed and accepted.

Gilbert Doucet, my character coach

Stand for something, or you will fall for everything. My dad has been my inspiration for standing for my own name, for who I am, and for what is the most valuable thing in my life: my character. Humble, yet dynamic and self-confident, he's the best example of a conscious businessman and a conscious human that I can ever hope to be.

Lorraine Doucet, my hope coach

My mom once sat with one of our family members who was depressed; she would sit with him for days not saying anything, just sitting there watching with soft eyes, accepting and sending her energy toward him. When I was at my lowest, I would go see her. She would just listen to me, not saying anything, not looking or judging. I didn't know what she was doing until I understood that she was just accepting me, loving me, and not judging me. She gave me hope in myself.

Diane Doucet (sister), my perseverance coach

Diane started Dovico by herself and built it into a brand. She then decided to homeschool her four children. She never gives up; she's tenacious and determined to leave everyone better than she found them. She's the example I need to get up and do more than I did yesterday.

Shelley Butler, my leadership coach

Shelley is my best friend, and she has never failed to understand my deepest of objectives, sometimes before I can even articulate them. Leadership requires acts of trust, acts of hope, and acts of love. Leadership is more acting than talking, more understanding than telling, and more caring than taking. Being around Shelley has and is constantly a push toward more of your capacity. She's the first to do the dishes, to serve the poor, and to call you on the intention of your action. I learned from her that the intention is more important than the business vision or mission.

Niki Butler, my inspiration coach

"Fall seven times, stand eight," is the quote Niki posted on Facebook the day I needed to stand up. I saw a young girl stand up and go to school despite the judgment, the naysayers, and the critics. She became my inspiration to get up and do something—anything—as long as it's something I believe in. She stood up in silence against her schoolmates, her teachers, her school, and the district. Then she went on to become the change she wanted to see in the world: a teacher. Oh, how lucky those kids will be … I wish I could be one of them.

Peter Dauphinee, my humble coach

When a conquering general or Caesar arrived in Rome after a great battle, the chariot always had a sage with Caesar who whispered, "You are just a man." This was to serve as a reminder to Caesar not to let the glory go to his head. Peter has been my mirror, my reflection; he's kept me humble while I've pursued the change I want to see in the world. He's told me what I didn't want to hear but needed to hear.

ACKNOWLEDGMENT

To Niki Butler, a student of life. She's been my inspiration not only to get up when I fell but also my friend. I want to thank her for the wonderful work as the editor.

To Jesse Dubberke, the creator of the art for this book, you've been a constant light in my life, and your creativity and innovation are inspirational.

ABOUT THE AUTHOR

It's impossible to change the world unless you inspire that change by changing yourself. Yves Doucet takes this statement to heart. As a genuinely inquisitive student of life, Yves puts great pride in sharing what he has learned, and he's always learning. You could call him a philanthropist of time. Yves puts considerable effort into helping others achieve, either through coaching, riveting conversation, or helping remove barriers that people create.

By official title, Yves is the business leader, owner and co-founder of a successful .com company but he would preferably be called a Culture Coach. As Dovico's Culture Coach, Yves helps his team find their passion and matches it with business. He genuinely believes that if the team is working aligned with their values, there is no obstacle to ingenuity and growth—both personally and professionally.

Yves' ambition in life is to make every day and everyone a little better than the way he found them. It's this energetic passion that makes his time and life meaningful and an influencer of change.

Professional engineer, certified Baptise yoga instructor, author, public speaker, entrepreneur, and innovator of tech companies.

You can reach Yves at www.yvesdoucet.com

Yves' Work and Communities

Dovico

At the beginning of his career, Yves worked as director and engineer at a research and development institute where they developed other people's ideas. The idea of an electronic timesheet came to him and his colleagues when they needed a better way to track and report on their time spent working on billable projects. In 1993, Dovico was born to develop the idea and offer it to others who had the same problem. Today, Dovico faithfully helps tens of thousands of people worldwide track their billable time. The growth of Dovico now provides gainful employment geared to not only a healthy income but healthy and productive lives.

www.dovico.com

ShowUp

The philosophy of Dovico centers around a famous expression: "If you want to go fast, go alone. If you want to go far, go together." This expression fits Dovico perfectly and has led to a new product called ShowUp. ShowUp is an innovative approach to empower individuals to grow personally inside of a professional team. This application was built from nearly three decades of learning from the failures and successes of the culture at Dovico. Citing a need to help improve company culture the right way, Yves once again aims to share a solution to the growing problem of employee retention and misaligned teams. ShowUp helps build an engaged workforce.

www.showup.io
Facebook https://m.facebook.com/yves.doucet.79
Instagram
yves_doucet